FATHERHOOD FUNDAMENTALS

A TWO-PART GUIDE FROM FIRST-TIME PREGNANCY TO BABY'S FIRST YEAR

ALEX GRACE

© Copyright 2024 - All rights reserved.

The content contained within this book may not be reproduced, duplicated, or transmitted without direct written permission from the author or the publisher.

Under no circumstances will any blame or legal responsibility be held against the publisher, or author, for any damages, reparation, or monetary loss due to the information contained within this book, either directly or indirectly.

Legal Notice:

This book is copyright protected. It is only for personal use. You cannot amend, distribute, sell, use, quote, or paraphrase any part, or the content within this book, without the consent of the author or publisher.

Disclaimer Notice:

Please note the information contained within this document is for educational and entertainment purposes only. All effort has been executed to present accurate, up-to-date, reliable, complete information. No warranties of any kind are declared or implied. Readers acknowledge that the author is not engaged in the rendering of legal, financial, medical, or professional advice. The content within this book has been derived from various sources. Please consult a licensed professional before attempting any techniques outlined in this book.

By reading this document, the reader agrees that under no circumstances is the author responsible for any losses, direct or indirect, that are incurred as a result of the use of the information contained within this document, including, but not limited to, errors, omissions, or inaccuracies.

CONTENTS

BOOK 1: YOU WILL ROCK
AS A DAD!

BOOK 2: YOU WILL ROCK AS A DAD!

BOOK 1: YOU WILL ROCK AS A DAD!

THE EXPERT GUIDE TO FIRST-TIME PREGNANCY AND EVERYTHING NEW FATHERS NEED TO KNOW

Alex Grace

INTRODUCTION

"The power of a dad in a child's life is unmatched."

— JUSTIN RICKLEFS

You've been wanting to be a father ever since you can remember. You always thought it would happen one day in the future. When your wife suggested it was time to start trying to get pregnant, you didn't hesitate. Most couples sometimes struggle to get pregnant, so you thought it could take at least a couple of months. "Trying to get pregnant will be fun," you thought, and "I'll have the most sex I've had in my whole life." These thoughts made you feel excited for the journey ahead.

Until one day, way sooner than you ever thought possible, your wife's waiting for you as you come home after a long day at work. You feel nervous looking at how excited she is. The next minute, she grabs a little white stick and points it so close to your face that you must step back to see what's happening.

You see two blue lines when your eyes eventually focus on the little stick (which now seems like it could be a weapon). What does this even mean? You wonder. Then, suddenly, you realize it might be a sign that your time of sex, whenever you wanted, was over. Carefully choosing your words, you ask, "Does this mean...." Before you can even finish your sentence, your wife shouts, "We're pregnant!"

Suddenly, a wave of emotions hit you. Feelings you can't understand. You always anticipated this to be the happiest day of your life. You have wanted this, so why would you not be ecstatic? But, apart from the apparent feelings of elation, you're suddenly overcome by feelings of extreme fear.

Thoughts are streaming through your head. What if something goes wrong? What if we don't have enough money to raise a child? What if I'm going to be a bad father? I don't know anything about being a dad. What if I can't console my baby when they cry? What if I do something that wrecks my child's life forever? The list of fears and thoughts mull through your head for weeks while you try to put on a brave face. The last thing you want is for your wife to realize that you're petrified at the thought of becoming a father.

If you've nodded in agreement to any of these fears, there's hope. You don't have to go through the next nine months (or the lifetime of being a father after that) alone. You don't have to wonder why your wife is seemingly impossible while pregnant. You don't have to fear the birth process. There's also no reason why you should be afraid of bringing the baby home, bonding with them, or being a good father.

Your fears will soon be a thing of the past. You've come to the right place. You Will Rock As a Dad! will help you through every step of the journey that lies ahead. It'll be the buddy you wish you could ask all the questions over a cold beer but feel too embarrassed to admit these fears to. This book—or buddy, if you will—will never judge you for being scared or asking what you fear might be silly questions.

Instead, this book will give you the support you need during these coming months. It'll help you know what to expect in every step of this pregnancy journey and having a newborn baby to care for. Many dads struggle to connect with their new babies, as they haven't physically carried the baby through pregnancy or given birth. Many dads don't understand the strength of their fatherly instincts, as society tends to focus only on the mother and their instincts in caring for a baby.

Apart from this, you'll need to find a new way of connecting to your wife, as your baby will become her highest priority. Then, you'll also need to find a way to make time for self-care. You'll need to carve time to do things yourself and not just settle into your new routine as a dad.

All of this can be enough to freak many men out, but you don't have to be one of them. There's no need to fear this time. Even though you might feel overwhelmed at times, you'll be ready for them. You Will Rock As a Dad! will also help you to know when your mental health might start to suffer and how to receive support.

ABOUT ME

I'm very excited to be helping you along your new journey. As a sports coach, my life is all about teamwork and collaboration. I'm the eldest in a family of five and have always been the fun uncle. But being the go-to family member for your nieces and nephews is nothing like having your own child. Even if you believe you'll be the best dad and love spending time with little ones, the shock of becoming a father can spin your head into such a loop that you might want to work out or do whatever helps blow off some steam and release some cortisol.

Your experience doesn't have to be like this. Helping parents, particularly new dads, find their feet in their new roles is one of my passions. I have a deep love for children, and after working in the childcare system for many years, I understand the attention to detail caring for a child requires. I have experience working with children from many backgrounds, which gives me different perspectives to draw knowledge from. I also have experience in fatherhood, having had the honor of becoming a dad a couple of times and creating my own little sports team at home.

I'm passionate about sharing my knowledge and experience because I know the value this can bring to first-time fathers. So, let's get straight into it and discuss what you should do and know when your wife announces her tummy is about to blow up like a balloon.

BONUS

Before we officially begin our journey together, I wanted to give you something.

As you embark on this exciting adventure, I understand that there are many questions and uncertainties that will arise, especially when it comes to supporting your partner through the miraculous process of labor and delivery.

To help you navigate this transformative experience with confidence and grace, I wanted to personally offer you a complimentary guide that I've made based on my first hospital trip experience and everything I wish I had brought.

In this comprehensive guide, you'll find practical advice, valuable insights, and items that will be the ultimate hack as you support your partner through labor and delivery.

Inside this guide, you'll discover:

- Hygiene items you didn't even think of bringing
- Ways to keep an eye on your baby at all times
- Nursing hacks to make the post-birth as smooth as possible
- Clothes your baby would thank you for if they could talk
- Comfort items to make everyone happy

Simply scan the QR code below to unlock your free copy of "The New Dad CheatSheet: The Ultimate 14 Essentials To Your Baby's Birth Hospital Trip" and start getting ready to be a dad.

Let's dive in.

CHAPTER ONE

YOU'RE GOING TO BE A DAD!

Y ou've had enough time to get over the initial shock that your wife's pregnant. At times, you're feeling quite pleased with yourself. After all, this is the best proof ever that your penis does work. Congratulations!

Despite this, you find yourself lying awake at night. You're scared of what lies ahead. Your life is no longer going to revolve around you. Sure, you had to make some adjustments when you got married or entered into a serious relationship with your partner. But, there was always still enough time to go out with the boys or do whatever you felt like. No matter what many people might try to tell you, this is about to change. This is scary. However, the more you educate yourself on the journey that you're embarking on, the less overwhelmed you'll feel.

HAVING A CHILD IS SCARY

Before we go over the nitty-gritty of pregnancy and caring for a newborn, let's focus on you and what you're likely going through. We've already established two emotions you might be feeling: happiness, maybe more delight and elation, and being so scared that you might even have to run to the toilet more often than usual. Sometimes, you're probably feeling both of those opposing emotions at the same time. Unfortunately for most dads-to-be, the fears of having a pregnant wife often outweigh the happiness or excitement of becoming a father.

You might fear that you're too selfish to be a good dad. Another person's needs will now become more important than your own. You won't be able to be selfish any longer. You'll have to devote hours daily to your family: You'll need to bond with your child, care for this new life, and take care of their mama, whose body will go through absolute hell over these upcoming months. Your time is no longer your own.

Similarly, you'll have to share your money. Having a baby's expensive, and there are just no two ways to avoid that. Diapers alone can break the monthly budget, not to mention all the other things your baby might need, such as formula, creams, medicine, doctor's appointments, clothes, daycare, and so on. Just as your priorities with your time will change, so will your financial responsibilities.

Fortunately, there's a silver lining to this. Many women (especially grandmas and aunts) are attracted to a baby like a magnet. If you need to have a break and have some selfish me-time, give these lovely women in your life a call to ask them to babysit or help your wife. Your wife might even want alone time from you. So do this, or at the very least, discuss this with her.

Like many, a woman's time can seem endless when cooing over a baby, and so can her purse. Have you ever seen a woman in a baby shop? Many tend to go crazy about blowing the budget by buying goodies. If you make sure someone gifts your wife with an oversized baby shower, you'll save a lot of money. Your baby will likely receive so many clothing items or packets of diapers that you might not have to buy as much for your baby as you fear. Make sure to keep the tags on all the clothing items your baby might receive so you can swap them out for different sizes if you need to.

Another fear you might have is loving your job more than your baby. Having this fear is more natural than you might realize. You've been doing your job for many years. You've chosen your career path. You might love your job so much that hours at work can feel like only a couple of minutes. Or maybe you don't like your job all that much. Perhaps you feel like you'll love hanging out with the guys more. This can still apply to you. Now, think back to when you started your first job or when you first met your best friend. Were you not scared of the unknown and failing? Looking back now, those fears seem pretty ridiculous, don't they? The same applies to having your first baby. You don't know what it's like to have your tiny human. You don't realize how you'll be entirely overcome by love the first time you hold your baby. As much as you love your job, your love for your baby will be completely different. Believe me, there's space in your heart for both.

A big fear of many dads-to-be is that they won't be a good father. Be kind to yourself. You don't have any experience in being a dad. It's so clichéd to say that you should follow your instincts, but it's true. If ever you don't know what to do, remember there can be many people in your life you can ask for advice. This can be a friend who already has kids, your parents, a co-worker, or your baby's doctor. Also, brace yourself now for the unrequested advice even strangers in the park or the mall will be all too happy to hand out. As much as some of these pieces of advice can be helpful, you'll learn to take them with a pinch (or sometimes a whole bag) of salt. What works for some parents might not work for you and your wife. You'll find your own rhythm when it comes to parenting.

A lot of dads-to-be fear they will lose their identity once they become a parent. When your wife reaches the end of her pregnancy and after the baby's born, your free time will become less. This means that you won't have as much time to spend on your favorite hobbies, hanging out with your buddies, or playing your favorite sports. You will now be a dad 24/7. This can change your sense of being; however, this can sometimes even be for the better. Having a baby forces you to mature to the next level, and you'll find other interests involving your child or being a parent. Also, remember that even though being a parent is a lifelong commitment to your child, not having as much time for what you used to do won't be a permanent change. Your child will grow up and become more independent, meaning your time will eventually free up again. Trust me when I say that time flies faster than you'd expect with your child. So, enjoy every step of the journey.

Many parents-to-be (not just dads) will experience a fear of missing out (FOMO), not only while pregnant but possibly for the first couple of years of their child's life. Let's quickly face this truth: You'll miss out on many things. Your life won't be carefree anymore, so you will not be able to drop everything to join your childless friends for a night out or a weekend away. While missing out on those exciting events, you'll gain a new excitement for raising your little human. Seeing your baby take their first step or hearing them say their first word will more than make up for the fun you might have had with friends. Your life will now be filled with memorable, once-in-a-lifetime moments. If you have a sound support system, you also don't have to miss out on seeing the people you care about. Once your child is old enough to sleep out, allow them to spend the night with someone you trust. You'll likely find that you and your wife will enjoy these odd nights out much more than before you had a child, and the following day when you pick the baby up, you'll probably be so happy to see them that you might not even moan about cleaning a dirty diaper.

Lastly, many soon-to-be dads fear getting what is often called the "dad bod." As much as this is a generalized joke, not all fathers pick up extra weight or get a "beer belly." As your family grows, your time for doing exercise will get less.

However, if you're strict about being active and not adding any inches around your waistline, you'll be able to achieve this. As your child grows, they will be able to join in your exercise routine. And before that, there's no rule stating you can't use your older baby or toddler as weight. Imagine your child is a 15-pounder dumbbell, and get those biceps working. Your child's giggles as you lift them up and down might motivate you to do more.

THINGS ALL MODERN DADS SHOULD KNOW

Now that you've faced some of the fears keeping you up at night let's delve deeper into your fear of not being a good dad. Just as your wife's body was made to give birth to a baby, your body was designed to be a dad. Want some proof? A study showed specific physiological and neurological changes in a man's body shortly before he becomes a dad (McKay, 2013).

One of the most significant signs is your testosterone levels. To help you become more nurturing, your testosterone levels will drop by about a third around three weeks before your baby's due (McKay, 2013). Don't worry. This won't affect your manliness forever. These levels will rise again to normal levels around six weeks after your baby's birth—coincidently, around the same time, most doctors recommend it is safe for mom to become sexually active again. Happy days are coming! Also, impress your wife with your extensive knowledge by throwing in this fact during a conversation. She'll be impressed, and you'll look like a super dad in the making.

With your testosterone dropping, your brain will become more tuned to a baby's crying as well. This proves the excuse of not hearing the baby crying at night is invalid. Sorry guys!

Also, remember that every dad-to-be handles pregnancy and the birth of their baby differently. While some men are amazed to see their partners pushing the baby through the birth canal, others fear seeing this might have a lasting effect on their desire for their partners. If you fall into this group, don't let that cause you stress. You might be so amazed by what your wife's body is capable of during childbirth that your love and desire for her can shoot through the roof. Remember that you don't have to watch the birth of your baby up close. You can stand by her head and support her through it. When you hear your baby cry, the wonder of childbirth will be over.

If you felt queasy looking at newborn photos online, that is okay. Newborns are often covered with vernix caseosa (the creamy white stuff we'll discuss later), excess hair, and blood. They are not always the picture-perfect sight you'll see in movies. Don't let the fear of being disgusted by the look of your baby freak you out and put you in a negative mindset. The nursing staff will clean all of that off. You might even be so overcome by pride and love for your baby that you won't care how they look. Always remember you're biologically designed to love and care for your baby. The proof is, as we've mentioned in the research.

As you're preparing yourself mentally for the arrival of your baby, parents-to-be need to consider their finances. Speak to friends with babies and ask how their babies have affected their budgets. Look at how much diapers, formula, creams, and other necessities cost and plan how you can fit all of that into your budget. If you need to cut back on certain aspects, start doing this now, so you're used to the changes before your baby's born. If you can, buy some big-ticket items such as a crib, changing table, and pram early on in the pregnancy so you can free up some money closer to when your baby's born. If money is tight, you don't have to buy these items new. Babies use these items for a short time, and you can find preloved items in excellent condition.

While getting yourself ready to be a father, managing your expectations is essential. Not all babies are happy or calm, and some are tiny terrors. Make peace with the fact that your baby might be a little tyrant. If you're mentally preparing yourself for this, your frustration levels will likely be lower when your baby cries for two hours straight than if you expect to have a perfect baby who never cries. I've never heard of a baby who doesn't cry. If your wife births a wonder like this, your baby might just make global news.

UNDERSTANDING YOUR MENTAL HEALTH AS A NEW DAD

Managing your expectations can go a long way in preserving your mental health through this journey of becoming a parent. The fears and worries mentioned above can severely impact a dad-to-be's mental health, so it's important to acknowledge when your mental wellness suffers and to always take care of yourself. Most men will also be reluctant to discuss the decline in their mental health with their partners. How can you moan about your anxiety while your wife's hurling in the toilet from morning sickness (that lasts all day long)? She might even scowl at you mid-vomit, saying something like: You did that to her. Fellas, don't take this personally. She's feeling miserable.

Choose a rare moment where she isn't losing her breakfast, lunch, or supper at the toilet to discuss your fears and anxiety with her. You might be surprised that she'll possibly share many of your worries. She's going through this pregnancy with you and may also feel unsure about how to care for your bundle of joy. Discussing your feelings can, therefore, help both of you.

If you feel that you can't discuss your anxiety with your partner or another friend, it's best to educate yourself as early in the pregnancy as possible, which is why you're reading this. The more you know and understand what is about to happen, the better you'll be able to prepare for it and the less anxiety you'll experience. Think of this as training before a big game. If you train 10 times harder now, you'll be more prepared and confident for the real thing.

Let's look at some of the significant stressors that can increase your anxiety (totally normal, by the way!) over the coming months:

Life changes

All changes can be scary, as it brings a lot of unknown factors. Since becoming a parent is a lifelong change, it can provoke even more anxiety. It can be helpful to surround yourself with other dads, as hearing them talk about their experiences can be helpful. You can also look at joining a Facebook group for new dads. They are your knowledge teammates in this.

Relationship changes

Your relationship with your partner will change. She'll go from not only being your lover but also being a mother. Your child will become her top priority. However, being parents can deepen the bond you two already share. Make sure you talk about things other than her pregnancy and the baby. Make sure you continue to date each other (even if these dates are in your pajamas on the couch at home).

Isolation

Especially during the first months after your baby has been born, you'll rush straight home after work to help your partner with the baby. At least for the first while, you won't be able to meet up with friends at a bar or go to a football game. This isolation can cause anxiety. Before becoming a dad, you were you first, so practice self-care as much as possible. Rope in the grandmas, grandpas, aunts, and uncles to help and escape for some selfish me-time when you need to. Do this for your wife, too, as you'll likely be way less grouchy when you return home.

Being the provider

We've mentioned the financial implications above. Being financially responsible for another life can provoke extreme anxiety. Make sure to plan and budget as much as you can. If need be, save money wherever you can. You might have to make peace with having a beer or two less a week. Have the funeral and mourn the loss of that beer. It'll be okay.

On a lighter note, now is the time to start memorizing some punchlines. No matter how lame your humor can be, the minute after your baby's born, you'll be officially qualified to tell your "dad jokes." Don't let anyone hold you back; unless your partner gives you a death stare. If so, stop. Immediately.

CREATING A BIRTH PLAN

To help ease your anxiety during this time, it can be helpful to start working on your wife's birth plan. This can help reduce the unknown factors increasing your feeling of not having control.

You'll soon begin attending prenatal visits to a doctor, so it's important to discuss this birth plan with the healthcare professional. You should also remember that things might not always go exactly according to plan, but that isn't something you should worry about yet.

Discuss the birth plan with your partner to make sure both of your wishes are included there. Once you get closer to the end of the pregnancy, make four copies of the plan: a copy to keep in your wife's hospital bag, another to keep on you, a copy for the doctor, and one for the hospital or center where she'll give birth.

Ask your partner the following questions to compile your birth plan:

- Do you want a home birth? Do you want to deliver at an out-of-hospital birth center? Or do you want to give birth in the hospital?
- Who do you want in the delivery room?
- Do you want to use a specific style of birthing? Examples here can include water, hypnobirthing, or Lamaze. If a cesarean section (C-section) is necessary, do you have any specific requests?
- Do you want a birthing coach or doula present?
- Do you want to use pain management? If so, what type of pain management?
- Do you want specific music played during delivery?
- Do you have special lighting requests?
- Who do you want to cut the umbilical cord?
- Do you want the umbilical cord cut as soon as possible, or do you want to delay cutting the cord?
- Are you going to breastfeed the baby? If so, do you want to feed the baby immediately after birth?
- Do you want skin-to-skin contact? Do you want me to do skin-to-skin contact with the baby? Do you want to bank cord blood? If so, what arrangements have you made?
- Do you want to keep the placenta? If so, what arrangements have you made?
- Who must be the first person you let know once the baby's born? Add their numbers to the list.
- How do you want to let people know you're parents?

- Will you send a photo to people to announce the birth?
- How long do you want to wait before you allow visitors in? Who do you want to visit first?

Once you've completed your birth plan, make copies and prepare them. As the pregnancy progresses, specific aspects of the birth plan might change. Simply make copies again every time things change. It's better to be prepared than to wait for the final draft and only realize on your way to the hospital with a wife in labor that you still need to print it or make copies.

If you have this ready and communicate with the obstetrician-gynecologist (OB-GYN) and hospital, you'll feel much more relaxed and prepared for what is to come. Your anxiety will decrease, and you'll be able to focus on other aspects of the pregnancy, spoiling your wife or sneaking in a quick game with a friend.

PRACTICAL NEW DAD TIP

Talk to your partner as often as possible. It sounds so cliché, but it's never encouraged enough. You're both going through something extraordinary yet utterly uncharted, so communicating your feelings to your partner will help you bond even more. When talking to your partner, be open about what you're feeling and start the conversation with "I" statements, such as "I am feeling nervous about being a bad dad" or "I am scared of not having enough money to care for the baby." This way, you're making yourself vulnerable and opening the conversation so she can either reassure you or let you know she has the same fears and you're not alone.

You can even turn this into a little game where you each take turns saying something you're feeling. This is an excellent way for both of you to discuss things causing anxiety. This will probably start superficially with statements such as, "I am excited about becoming a parent." Make sure to bring some depth in by addressing real concerns. This might make you realize that your partner is also having a rough time. Have lines such as, "I am excited to parent with you," or "I am looking forward to seeing what an amazing mom you'll be," ready to reassure her during these conversations.

If you don't want to start smack-bam with deep feelings or want brownie points, open the conversation with a line like, "I am nervous about what your body will go through during the pregnancy." This way, you're addressing one of your emotions while also showing her that you care about what she's going through. A double win right there!

Be sensitive to her needs during these conversations. Make sure she's comfortable, and don't make a face or sarcastic comment if she interrupts you mid-sentence for yet another pee break. She can't help it. Since she shouldn't be drinking alcohol while pregnant, avoid the urge to crack open a beer for yourself during this talk. Having these types of conversations is something you'll have to learn to do without any liquid courage.

CHAPTER TWO

SUPPORT HER

Now that we've addressed some of your fears and causes for anxiety, let's turn our focus to the most important person for the next nine months: the mom-to-be. Her

body will go through various changes, from raging hormones that result in her turning from your loving wife to a Tyrannosaurus rex within the blink of an eye, the weirdest cravings (think of a hamburger with condensed milk and sardines on it), to having a belly that is about to grow so big that she won't be able to see her toes anymore. How beautiful is it that your child is literally growing inside of her? How freaking cool is that?!

While she's going through all these changes, the fear of childbirth will be ever-present. She'll either have to endure excruciating pain pushing an 8 lb baby out of her body, or she'll have to undergo major surgery to remove them from her tummy and then be forced to get up and walk around hours after the surgery to care for it. Regardless, I'm sure most women will agree with me; childbirth is no joke.

There will likely be times during the pregnancy when you'll feel powerless, as there isn't much you can do to make any of this easier. However, understanding more about what she's going through mentally, emotionally, and physically will go a long way in ensuring a happy pregnancy for both of you.

SEX AND BODY CHANGES DURING PREGNANCY

Let's first discuss the changes that her body will go through. One of the first symptoms she'll probably experience is swollen and painful boobs. Fellas, if you value your life, you shouldn't try to touch (or grab) them. Don't even hug her too tightly. In all seriousness, showing respect to your partner's body during this time is crucial. Happy wife = happy life.

Talking of sex unless there are complications in the pregnancy and your wife's doctor advises against it, it's usually completely safe to be intimate while pregnant. She might not feel up for it throughout the pregnancy and definitely won't want anything close to her fanny after giving birth. The bigger her belly gets, the less sexy she may feel. Her hormones might also cause her to rarely be in the mood. Sex will also become more uncomfortable as her tummy grows.

Another symptom that often manifests early in pregnancy is extreme nausea and vomiting called morning sickness. Don't let the name of this symptom fool you. This doesn't only happen during the morning. Nausea can hit your partner at any time of the day or stick around like a shadow all day, every day. Morning sickness usually shows its ugly head between six to eight weeks of pregnancy. The vomiting can also be completely unexpected, so your wife might throw up in front of you or even in the middle of a busy mall. Be prepared to assist in making her as comfortable as possible. She might want your help or just want some space. Communication is key here.

Instead of being disgusted by this (believe me, more disgusting things are waiting for you in the delivery room), help her by stocking up on crackers or ginger biscuits. Both of these are known to decrease the symptoms of nausea. Keep some next to the bed and ensure she eats one the minute she wakes up in the morning before moving around too much. This will help to settle her tummy slightly. If she's feeling sick, never ask her what's for dinner. Man up and cook your own food. Ask her if she wants to eat and, if so, what she wants. Should she be too sick, eat in another room, so she doesn't have to deal with the smell of your food. It might even help you enjoy your meal more, as you won't have to look at her fighting the urge to hurl. If her symptoms get very severe, take her to the doctor. There are many pregnancy-safe medications she can drink to alleviate this symptom. Dehydration is also possible in cases of severe vomiting, which can be dangerous to your wife and the baby. Make sure she drinks enough water!

Apart from what she throws up, you might feel confused by what she wants to eat. These cravings usually start during the first trimester of pregnancy but can peak at any time. They are caused by a combination of hormones, nutritional deficiencies, and an increased sense of taste and smell.

Humor her in any weird cravings she might have, and if she sends you out at midnight in search of donuts, be a good guy and get some for her. The couple of minutes of sleep you'll loose going out on the donut run will be worth it. Otherwise, you'll most likely lose sleep due to having a cranky partner in bed with you. Most food cravings are harmless, such as dairy products, fruit, pickles, or chocolate. If the combinations of foods she craves put you off, give her what she wants and leave the room while she enjoys it.

If her cravings are incredibly unhealthy, you can try to beat this by encouraging her to eat a healthy and well-balanced diet. These cravings are often a way for her body to ensure it gets the nutrients, such as iron or calcium, that the baby needs to grow. The cravings might subside if you advocate that she gets in everything she (and the baby) needs. If they are still there, give her what she craves, but keep things in moderation.

When discussing her cravings with her, choose your words carefully. Her hormones are raging, which can result in mood swings severe enough that you might want to run for the hills. Whatever you do, don't run! She's carrying another human being inside her, and her body is trying to figure out what's happening. She is literally producing a miracle inside of her. And, as much as she tries to, she can't control her hormones or moods most of the time. She might go from being the happiest mom-to-be one minute to crying uncontrollably the next. This is normal, particularly during the beginning and again towards the end of the pregnancy. Share in her excitement when she's happy, comfort her when she's crying (even if it's for no reason whatsoever), and listen while she vents.

If she forgets why she's crying or the cause of her anger is mid-sentence, don't rush to take her to the neurosurgeon for a brain scan or start planning dementia treatment. The hormone surge in her body and physiological changes in her brain can lead to what is often referred to as a pregnancy brain. She might become highly forgetful and struggle to complete tasks. Studies have found that pregnant women have less gray matter volume in the areas of the brain that deal with social skills and building relationships (Barth, 2020). Many believe this is how mama prepares for caring for her tiny human. It's also another pregnancy-related fact you can impress your wife with. You're on a roll here!

Dealing with pregnancy brain can be very frustrating, not just for you but also for your partner. Help her through this by being kind to her and making sure she gets enough sleep, drinks enough water, and plays games that can boost her brain function.

Stress and anxiety can also contribute to her feeling fuzzy and forgetful. Help her to relieve stress by talking with her about her fears, making lists of things that should be done, or giving her massages to help her relax. Who knows what these massages might even lead to...Probably a good night's sleep for you both! I don't know what you were thinking, but not everything has to be dirty or about sex. Come on now, dad-to-be!

KEEP DATING YOUR WIFE AND PLAN A BABYMOON

This is the last time you and your wife can go on dates without needing to arrange a babysitter. Soon, you might feel like you're a teenager again, needing to ask your mom (or your babysitter) for permission to go out. Use this time. Plan romantic dates. But do it without having any expectations of a happy ending. Your wife might not be in the mood or too uncomfortable to do the horizontal dance. However, being romantic and showing her that you love and appreciate her will go a long way in improving your odds.

If you want to get the badge of husband of the year, plan a last getaway for just you and your partner before your baby's born. This little vacation is often called a babymoon and will be the last time you can relax together before becoming parents. When planning this getaway, keep your wife's condition in mind. She won't be able to consume any alcohol or sushi or do anything adventurous.

Now isn't the time to plan a bungee jumping or deep-sea-diving trip. Your swimmers have done enough already.

Instead, plan activities that both of you can enjoy. This can include a relaxing picnic, a stroll on the beach, sightseeing, or simply spending time indoors in each other's company. All your mom-to-be might want is a king-size bed (for sleeping!), an air conditioner (especially if she's pregnant during summer, as she'll likely feel like a heater), and room service. Alternatively, find out what your wife would like to do.

Make sure you plan this trip well. If you leave it too late during the pregnancy, you'll run the risk of your wife going into labor on location. The last thing either of you will want to do is search frantically for a hospital in a town neither of you knows. She might also develop a pregnancy-related complication causing her doctor to advise her against traveling. No matter when you plan this babymoon during the pregnancy, it'll be good to research that there's a good hospital nearby. Complications during pregnancy can come suddenly and unexpectedly. However, never fear the possibility of complications. You're getting ready with the correct helpful information and tips to be as prepared and confident as possible.

MENTAL HEALTH DURING AND AFTER PREGNANCY

Pregnancy, especially the first couple of months of parenthood, can be a rollercoaster ride, filled with hormones, emotions, and sleep deprivation for you and your partner. As we've mentioned in Chapter 1, this is why it's so important to constantly be looking out for your mental health and seeking the necessary support should you ever find your mental health declining.

The mood swings that come with being pregnant often affect the mental health of the pregnant woman and her partner. She might cry for no reason and get angry over things that usually wouldn't even phase her. This, combined with the stress of becoming a mom, can easily lead to anxiety and depression. The same goes for the dad-to-be. Your sweet wife can now seem like an emotional monster at times. This might cause you to feel helpless and like you can do nothing right.

The slippery slope to mental health issues like depression and anxiety during pregnancy can make this experience even scarier. This is why it's so important to talk as soon as you experience common symptoms, such as extreme stress and worry, sadness, loss of appetite (or sudden overeating), agitation, and lack of interest in things you enjoy.

As much as it's essential to be aware of your mental health during pregnancy, it's even more crucial to take care of yourself after the baby's born. You might have heard "baby blues" or "postpartum depression" before, but it's key to be aware of what exactly this means and what the signs are to look out for so either you or your partner can get the support you might need. Don't feel overwhelmed by the extensive terms and possible scary experiences. Instead, see this as simply becoming aware of the potential effects on your and your partner's mental wellness. Remember that through awareness and education, you gain knowledge and confidence.

Let's first discuss the mental health of the new mom. As much as she's excited about bringing a new life into the world, it might not always affect her as positively as many think. It's also much more common than people realize: One in eight new moms suffer from some sort of postpartum depression (Gomstyn, 2022). As you'll see below, the level of depression a new mom can experience varies from mild to severe.

- Baby blues. This is the most common mental health problem moms deal with after giving birth. The symptoms usually only last for a couple of days to two weeks:
- Sleeping problems
- Irritability
- Lack of concentration
- Anxiety
- Sadness and crying
- Lack of appetite
- Feeling overwhelmed

Postpartum depression. This is often regarded as baby blues when it starts, but the symptoms last longer and can be so severe that they can impair the mom's ability to perform daily tasks or care for the baby. Symptoms of postpartum depression don't always start right after childbirth; they can begin during pregnancy or up to a year of the baby being born:

- Feeling depressed
- Feeling hopeless, inadequate, or worthless
- Isolating from friends and family
- Inability to bond with the baby
- Constant crying
- Lack of energy
- Extreme irritability or anger
- Thoughts of harming herself and/or the baby

Postpartum psychosis. This condition is rare and can have life-threatening consequences if not treated. Symptoms usually start around a week after the baby's born:

- Disorientation and feeling confused
- Paranoia
- Extreme agitation
- Obsessive thoughts, particularly over the baby
- Hallucinations and delusions
- Attempts at harming herself and/or the baby

As mentioned above, postpartum depression can also affect new dads. Similar to how it can affect a new mom, being a depressed new father doesn't mean you're weak or a failure. It's a medical condition called paternal postpartum depression and has the same symptoms as what moms will experience. Research showed that around one in ten new fathers suffers from this mental health condition (Gomstyn, 2022). The following are known to be risk factors for new dads to develop paternal postpartum depression:

- History of depression or other mental health conditions
- Financial difficulties
- Problems in the relationship with your partner
- Being very young

We've already mentioned that having open discussions with your partner can help alleviate mild symptoms of depression and anxiety. However, if the symptoms last longer than two weeks after the birth of your baby, get worse, or impact your ability to care for your baby, you can benefit from seeking help from your primary care physician. There's no shame in seeking the support you need; instead, the shame lies in believing you don't need help and making this experience even tougher on you than it needs to be. Don't be that guy.

Get help if you need it. Help your partner if she's struggling. Be aware of what is going on and use the knowledge you've gained to act with confidence. The sooner you and your partner get the help you need, the better it'll be for your whole family, especially your new baby.

PRACTICAL NEW DAD TIP

Take your wife out on a date. That might be the last thing on both of your minds, as your thoughts are likely consumed by pregnancy and raising a child. However, that makes this the perfect time to show her you acknowledge how incredible this journey is that you're both embarking on. She'll be carrying your child for nine months. Let her know how absolutely special that is.

CHAPTER THREE

THE PRE-GAME WARM UP

Wohooo! You now have a much better understanding of what to expect during your wife's pregnancy.

You're aware of the changes her body is going through and to never judge or make remarks about any of her weird cravings. You also know to always look out for signs of anxiety and depression in her and yourself.

While having overall knowledge of what lies ahead is good, it's just as important to understand the different trimesters of pregnancy and what to expect during each of them. The nine months or forty weeks of pregnancy are divided into three trimesters, although many professionals advocate that the first three months of a baby's life should be regarded as the fourth trimester— another fact you can impress your wife with. Let's start at the beginning and discuss all you should know about the first trimester or the pre-game warm-up of pregnancy.

THE FIRST TRIMESTER OF PREGNANCY

As you might already know or could guess (kudos to you), the first trimester of pregnancy is the earliest stage of pregnancy (or weeks 1 to 13). The weeks of pregnancy are counted from the first date of a woman's last menstrual period before getting pregnant, so the count starts before actually getting pregnant.

Pregnancy symptoms can differ from woman to woman and even from pregnancy to pregnancy. If she's having a tough pregnancy now, it doesn't mean future pregnancies will be the same. In general, the first trimester isn't always the most pleasant time for the mom-to-be. Her body goes through the shock of hormones and drastic changes to get ready to house your tiny human for nine months. As we've mentioned, she might start to experience morning sickness, sore boobs, mood swings, and cravings, but there are many other symptoms associated with the first trimester:

Spotting

Stay calm if your wife comes to you freaking out about bleeding down there. Excessive bleeding can be a sign of miscarriage (we'll discuss that as well), but a degree of slight bleeding can be expected. This is often called implantation bleeding and is simply a result of the embryo implanting in her uterus. Never make a face when she shows you bleeding or other discharge on toilet paper. As gross as it might be for you to see, she's probably freaking out. If there are any concerns about any form of bleeding, it's always best to consult with her doctor.

Discharge

While on the topic of what might show on toilet paper after she wipes, excess discharge is also very common. As long as this discharge is thin and milky, it's perfectly fine. However, call the doctor if it ever turns yellow or green and has a strong smell. Again, avoid calling this discharge "gross" or telling her how badly it smells. Instead, be a good husband and go buy her some pantyliners to help relieve the discomfort any discharge can cause.

Constipation

The hormone increase in her body can slow down the muscle contractions that move food through her digestive system, resulting in excessive gassiness, bloatedness, and constipation. Ensure she eats enough fibers and drinks plenty of water to help with this. Unless your relationship is on that level of comfortableness, never make fun of her or comment on the sound or odor if she farts in front of you. If you value your life and relationship, pretend it never happened.

Fatigue

The first trimester of pregnancy can take a toll on her body, causing extreme fatigue. Let her have a nap while you do some of her household chores. Never make her feel guilty about needing to nap or even comment about the number of naps she has taken in a day. Most importantly, never complain about how tired you might be. Trust me, she's at least 10 times more tired than you.

Frequent Urination

Your wife will be peeing a lot more than ever before. Her uterus is expanding rapidly to make space for the growing baby, putting a lot of pressure on her bladder. Make sure your partner doesn't cut down on fluids because of this. Her body will need the fluids to grow your child. Instead, show her you care by stocking up on more toilet paper. If you don't usually use it, go for two-ply. The skin down there will get more sensitive as the pregnancy progresses, so spending a little bit more money on toilet paper will make her life much more pleasant.

Heartburn

This is a common problem many pregnant women complain about during pregnancy, and hormones can again take the blame for this. To help her relieve these symptoms, let her eat smaller meals throughout the day and avoid greasy food. If it gets so bad that she struggles to eat, consult with a doctor. There are many medications she can use that are safe to take during pregnancy.

BABY'S GROWTH

Even though your wife's tummy will likely not show during the first trimester, the changes in her uterus are remarkable. In these few weeks, your baby will go from being a fertilized egg to a fully formed fetus. The major organs in your baby's body will start to form. Let's look at some of these developments:

The baby's nervous system will begin forming with an open tube from the brain to the spinal cord.

At around six weeks of pregnancy, you might be able to hear the baby's heartbeat on an ultrasound scan. It beats very fast: between 120 to 160 beats per minute (Watson, 2020a). Your heart will likely beat faster with excitement hearing this for the first time.

The baby's soft skeleton begins to grow with a digestive system, including the kidneys and intestines. The lungs will also form but won't fully develop until the third trimester.

The baby can move its muscles, and you'll be able to see this on an ultrasound scan, but your wife won't feel these movements just yet.

Towards the end of the first trimester, your fetus will start to look like a little baby, with a face, tongue, tooth buds, eyelids, fingernails, and genitals. In most cases, these genitals will still be too small to be able to tell the gender of the baby just yet.

By around 13 weeks, your baby will be about 3 in. long (Watson, 2020a).

You should be amazed by reading all of these changes your wife's body creates in the baby. Show this by treating her to something that she really enjoys, even if it's just a quiet, clean, and neat home where she can rest. After cleaning, use this as an excuse to do something you enjoy.

If you want to impress your partner with your extensive knowledge of her pregnancy, there are many places you can get weekly updates on what to expect during that week of her pregnancy and the baby's size and development. You can register on many baby websites to receive weekly emails or download apps on your smartphone to track the pregnancy.

PRENATAL VISITS, EXERCISE, AND OTHER TIPS

A couple of things should be done during the first trimester.

Impress your partner with your knowledge on this, make a to-do list, and take it one thing at a time. The more things you tick off your list, the more you'll be able to relax and enjoy this journey.

At the top of your list should be finding a doctor for your wife. The specialist who deals with pregnancies, childbirth, and postpartum care is an obstetrician, and a gynecologist deals with, amongst others, the reproductive health of women. A doctor who combines both these specialties is called an obstetrician-gynecologist. Get the best of both worlds by listing all the OB-GYNs in your area. By opting for a doctor specializing in both fields, your wife can also build a relationship with this person for future gynecological care.

Unless you live in a small town, you'll likely have a wide variety of OB-GYNs in your area to choose from. Find out which OB-GYNs are in your insurance network if you have health insurance. This will likely narrow your search down. If you have a preferred hospital, look at which specialists have surgical rights there. If your wife's still undecided about who to choose, talk to friends or colleagues who recently had babies about their experiences with their doctors, or search for reviews online.

Remember that the doctor's decision doesn't have to be set in stone. If your wife isn't happy with the chosen doctor, you can always move to another one. Even if you like the chosen doctor, this is about your wife and her care and not about who you prefer. Most OB-GYNs keep availability in their schedules for pregnant women, so you shouldn't struggle too much to get an appointment with a different doctor if need be.

Once your wife decides on a doctor, schedule an appointment. Most OB-GYNs prefer to see their patients toward the end of the first trimester and then every four weeks after that. Try your best to go with her to every appointment. The doctor will do an ultrasound scan at these appointments, so you can see your baby and track its development. The doctor will also check your wife's blood pressure, test her urine for proteins, and weigh her to keep track of weight gain. Fellas, however tempted you might be to sneak a peek at the scale, never ever do this. Soon, your wife will feel enormous and may even feel embarrassed about the weight she's gaining (even though all pregnant women should gain weight). Don't make this experience worse for her by looking. If you accidentally see her weight, never comment about it. If you say something like, "Wow, you're now 30 lb heavier than when we met," you might find yourself single soon. This may seem like common sense, but even common sense isn't always so common. Be her support, not the person who makes her feel uncomfortable or makes fun of her.

Next on the to-do list should be getting an excellent prenatal vitamin for your wife. During the first trimester, it's essential to look for a vitamin containing folic acid (at least 400 micrograms [μg]), as this holds many benefits for the development of your baby's brain and spinal cord (Watson, 2020a). During the second and third trimesters, prioritize that the prenatal vitamin your wife takes is high in omega-3.

If your partner is a smoker, now is a good time to quit this habit. If you also smoke, don't be that guy that smokes around a pregnant woman. As difficult as it might seem, try and quit with her. It won't be easy for her either. Getting rid of this bad habit now will also make this easier once your baby's born, as you don't want to come close to a newborn baby smelling of smoke.

Alcohol is another big no-no while pregnant. If mama craves beer or wine, look for the non-alcoholic options in your local liquor store. She should also cut down on caffeine. It's widely believed that one cup of coffee daily is safe, so make sure one cup is delicious so she can enjoy every sip.

Moderate exercise is important during pregnancy. This will help to keep the mom-to-be healthy, limit excess weight gain, promote your baby's health, and reduce stress and anxiety. Discuss the exercises your wife's planning on doing with her doctor. Especially during the early stages of pregnancy, walking, swimming, yoga, and low-impact aerobics classes are generally considered safe. Things she should avoid are picking up heavy weights and exercises where she might fall. Make this a fun couples activity by joining your wife in working out. It might also be a great bonding opportunity for the two of you; as the saying goes, "A couple who sweat together, stay together." (DiDonato, 2014)

Another thing to consider is breaking the good news to the people you care about. There's no right or wrong time to tell your loved ones. Some people spread the news the minute they get a positive reading on a pregnancy test. Others wait until after their first prenatal doctor's appointment, while many wait to share the excitement at the beginning of the second trimester, as the risk of miscarriage will decrease as the pregnancy progresses. Most companies require pregnant employees to inform human resources by 12 weeks, so remind your wife to double-check the policy at work.

WHEN TO RUSH TO THE DOCTOR

As much as you should never dwell on the negatives, it's essential to be aware of the signs that things might not go as planned. Understanding what to look out for will help you decide when to rush your partner to the doctor or when to put on calming music, give a relaxing massage, or run her a bubble bath.

Heavy bleeding

As we've mentioned above, minor spotting can be perfectly normal. However, if your wife ever experiences heavy bleeding, she should get checked out immediately, as this can signify a miscarriage.

Severe abdominal pain

Some abdominal pain can be expected during pregnancy as ligaments stretch, and her uterus expands to accommodate the growing baby. Should this pain ever become severe or sharp, it's best to have this checked out. This pain can be another sign of miscarriage or an ectopic pregnancy, where the fertilized egg grows outside her uterus.

Dizziness

Severe dizziness can be another sign of an ectopic pregnancy, which can then be a sign of low blood pressure. This is important to notice as if she gets so dizzy, she may faint, and this fall can hurt the baby.

Blurred vision

This can be a sign of gestational diabetes (abnormally high blood sugar) or preeclampsia, a condition caused by high blood pressure that also causes protein in her urine. Both of these conditions can result in severe complications for both your partner and the baby, so it's best to have it checked out.

DEEP DIVE EMOTIONS

Seeing your baby for the first time on an ultrasound scan and hearing its heartbeat can unlock a whole new flow of emotions: pride, excitement, elation, and the fear that we've discussed. Apart from discussing your emotions and fears, there are many things you and your partner can do together to make sure your mental health doesn't dive during this time:

Eat healthy, regular meals.

Try to do moderate exercise at least three to five times per week.

Be realistic about your expectations of what you, especially your wife, can do. Now isn't the time for her to try and be a superwoman. She's already using all her superpowers to grow the baby and is a real-life wonder woman.

Unless you have to, try not to make significant changes, such as moving house(s), during this time. Keep life as normal and stress free as possible.

Spend time with the people who are important to both of you, make you happy, and positively impact your life.

If possible, connect with other pregnant couples or couples who recently had a baby. Sharing your experiences and listening to what others went through can be extremely helpful and help to prepare you for all possible events. Keep in mind that not every experience will be the same. Don't let someone else's bad experience make you want to go sit in a dark corner and cry. Your adventure during pregnancy and childbirth might be completely different.

PRACTICAL NEW DAD TIP

Ask your partner what food she's craving or what she absolutely doesn't want anywhere close to her. Her body and hormones are changing, so letting her know you acknowledge that by asking what she wants to eat is an excellent way to support her and make her feel loved and appreciated.

CHAPTER FOUR

THE FIRST HALF

Boom! You've made it to the honeymoon stage of the pregnancy. The second trimester is usually considered the most fun for both mom and dad. The extreme sickness and fatigue she might have felt during the first trimester will soon be gone, and she'll have a couple of weeks' break before the extreme uncomfortableness of the growing baby will get her down during the third trimester. Now is a great time to go on that babymoon we discussed in Chapter 2.

Over the next couple of weeks, you will, if you choose to know, likely find out the gender of the baby. The baby's movements will also get stronger. First, your wife, and then you can feel the baby's kicks. Your wife's tummy will also grow, and the preggy belly will become more and more noticeable. Now is the time to work on bringing your A-game regarding guard duties. Strangers might randomly start touching your wife's tummy. This strange phenomenon will only get more extreme once the baby's born, as some will try to touch your precious tiny human. Keep your hand strong and ward off any unwanted affections.

YOU MADE IT THROUGH THE FIRST TRIMESTER

Your partner has made it through the pre-game warm-up and is now in the first half, AKA the second trimester of the pregnancy. This trimester starts in week 14 and continues until week 27. Although some bad symptoms, such as heartburn, your wife will likely start to feel much better and more energetic. Her boobs will probably also not be so sore anymore, and her increased estrogen levels might work in your favor, so your luck in getting her frisky might be up.

Since her energy levels should be up and her belly growing, why not take her on a nice shopping trip for maternity clothes? Her clothes won't fit for much longer, and if you wait till her tummy is peeking out her shirts, she might be too sore and uncomfortable to walk around in the mall. Help her on this trip. Don't stand around irritated at the shops' entrances or mall aisles waiting for your wife to get done. Help her to choose clothes, or surprise her with something she likes later at home.

As your baby grows, its movements will become more significant. Between 18 to 25 weeks, your wife will start to feel these movements. At first, it'll feel like fluttering but will soon become proper kicks. Only a couple of weeks after your wife starts to feel the first movements, you'll also be able to feel the karate kid's kicks. When looking at the week-by-week milestones during pregnancy, always keep in mind that every pregnancy progresses at its own pace. Yours might not be exactly as it is believed to be, so if you're ever concerned about milestones not being reached, discuss this with your OB-GYN.

Towards the end of the second trimester, your partner may start to struggle to get comfortable enough to fall asleep. Here are two more chances to impress your wife. Firstly, advise her to sleep as much as possible on her left side, as this increases the blood flow to her uterus. Secondly, and this can be quite an award-winning move for you, buy her a pregnancy pillow. This long, C-shaped pillow supports her head, neck, and growing belly and back. After the baby is born, this pillow can be just as handy for them to lay on during feeds. However, as the baby gets bigger, pack this pillow far away. Otherwise, your wife might just start to love and cuddle it more than you.

As the pregnancy progresses, you might notice changes in your partner's skin. Due to the increase in hormones, she might feel like she's a teenager again struggling with acne. Stretch marks may appear soon, particularly on her tummy, breasts, and bum. Never comment on these stretch marks; see them as another reminder of the miracle her body is busy creating. Vitamin E oil can help to reduce the appearance of these marks and is safe to use during pregnancy.

She might also develop dark marks on her face called melasma and a dark line down the middle of her stomach called linea nigra. These changes should fade and eventually disappear after the baby's born. Apart from this, her skin will become more sensitive. Make sure to rub her with sunscreen that has an SPF of at least 30 when she goes outside.

Towards the end of this trimester, your partner can experience pains in her lower abdomen. This is due to her expanding uterus, which puts extra pressure on and stretches her ligaments and muscles. She might also have backache(s) caused by the excess weight she's carrying around her belly. Take out the vitamin E oil and use it again to give her a relaxing massage.

Many pregnant women experience bleeding gums, and this is due to hormones causing the gums to swell. If your wife suffers from this, get her a toothbrush with softer bristles to use in the meantime, and remind her to be gentler when she flosses her teeth. Nosebleeds are also more common during pregnancy, as the hormones can cause the mucus membranes in the nose to swell. This can even cause your wife to start snoring. Don't mock her for snoring. Help her by getting a pregnancy-safe decongestant or saline drop to alleviate the buildup in her nose.

The second trimester is a good time to look into birthing or antenatal classes. This will help you prepare for what to expect in the delivery room, how to help your wife through labor, what will happen after your baby's birth, and how to care for your baby once you take your new family member home. Most importantly, this will help you realize you won't break the baby by picking them up, that it's perfectly fine and manly to be goofy around your child, and that you're allowed to brag as much as possible.

If you want to up your fatherly game now, look into how to take the best photos or videos of a newborn. Mom will be busy nursing or caring for the baby, and one of your first jobs will be to take as many photos as possible. Eventually, photos, videos, and your memories will be all you'll have of your baby's first couple of days, so make sure not to fumble your first duties of fatherhood. Instead, secure yourself a badge of honor by capturing the first days as best you can.

SIZE OF YOUR BABY

While your wife's experiencing all these changes, your baby's growing at a steady pace. Many of the baby's organs are now fully formed, and the baby can swallow, suck, open their eyelids, hiccup, and hear your voice. By this stage, your baby will even have its own fingerprints. The baby will start to go through cycles of being awake and sleeping.

Since your baby's in amniotic fluid, fine hair called lanugo, and a vernix caseosa, a creamy, white coating covers the baby's entire body. This protects the baby's skin from being constantly in the fluid. This vernix is absorbed by the skin, and babies born after their due date will likely not have any traces of vernix on their skin at birth.

By the end of the second trimester, your baby should be around 3 pounds and 16 inches long, around the size of an English cucumber (Watson, 2020b).

BABY'S GENDER

Finding out the gender of your little bundle of joy is another exciting part of pregnancy. Some people prefer to wait until the baby is born and get the surprise in the delivery room, while others want to find out what they are expecting as soon as possible. Knowing what you're expecting can make it easier to prepare for the baby's arrival if you want to use traditional gender colors in the baby's room or clothes.

Unless the baby's in a difficult position during your ultrasound scan, most OB-GYNs can determine the gender of the baby between 16 to 20 weeks, although it can sometimes be seen on the scan as early as 14 weeks. The OB-GYN will generally look for the presence of a penis. If a penis can be seen on the scan, the doctor will quickly tell you it's a boy. However, this isn't always accurate. If your baby's a late bloomer, or if the penis is hidden behind the umbilical cord or between the legs, you might think you're expecting a girl, only to get the surprise later on.

Tell the doctor if you want to keep the baby's gender a surprise. Should you wish to find out, decide how you'd like this to happen.

Some couples ask the OB-GYN to tell them during an ultrasound scan, while others want to find out surrounded by the people they care about during a gender reveal party.

If you want to do a party, you can ask your OB-GYN to write the gender of the baby on a piece of paper, closed in an envelope. This can then be handed to whoever is helping to keep the gender secret. Some people like to put either blue or pink feathers in a dark balloon that the pregnant couple must pop to reveal the gender, while others have a color-themed cake made, where the gender is revealed once the cake is cut. However you decide to do it, make sure you have the right equipment. You don't want to stand forever trying to pop a balloon with a blunt needle. It's also best not to have this balloon filled with helium, as you might accidentally release the balloon into the sky while still getting ready to pop it. If this happens while a family member records you, you might become the butt of a joke going viral on social media.

Apart from seeing the penis (or lack of a penis) on the ultrasound scan, other tests can help to identify the gender. Since these tests are often not done routinely and can carry some risks, most OBGYNs wouldn't advise doing them simply to determine the gender of the baby. These tests include:

Amniocentesis

This is done to detect developmental issues in a fetus, such as Down syndrome and spina bifida. A long needle is inserted into the womb to withdraw amniotic fluid. Tests done on this fluid can show the gender of the baby. It does, however, bring a risk of miscarriage, so it's only done if there's a significant concern over the baby's development.

Chorionic villus sampling

This is another test done to diagnose Down syndrome in an unborn baby. Through this test, a sample of the placenta is removed. It shows the genetic information of the baby, which includes the gender of the baby. This test also carries the risk of miscarriage and preterm labor.

Non-invasive prenatal test

This blood test checks for the possibility of a chromosomal disorder. It's usually done if you're at high risk of giving birth to a baby with a chromosome abnormality.

PRACTICAL NEW DAD TIP

Ask your partner if she'd like to do a gender reveal party. It can be a great way to bring the families together and celebrate another milestone for your soon-to-be little human. Decide whether you want to arrange this party yourself or if you want to ask a family member or friend to host it. Remember to make sure the way you'll reveal the gender is foolproof.

CHAPTER FIVE

THE SECOND HALF

The home stretch of the pregnancy! The first trimester, stretching from weeks 28 to 40, or whenever the baby's born, can be the most taxing on the mom-to-be. To say

she'll be uncomfortable will be the understatement of the century. Even though this last trimester is only 12 weeks, it'll feel like a year for her.

Her tummy will be huge, her legs will likely swell, she'll be tired from running to the bathroom all the time, and as much as people will advise her to sleep before the baby comes, she'll struggle for most of the night to get comfortable enough to fall asleep. If she does get comfortable, she'll likely only get to lay like that for a minute or two before she needs to rush to the bathroom for yet another pee break. Your baby will be using her bladder as a trampoline, bouncing around in her uterus like a true gymnast. Every time this happens, your wife will need to run (or waddle) to the bathroom as soon as possible.

If things ever get so rough that you feel like drowning yourself in the toilet bowl, remind yourself that in only a couple of weeks, everything you've been going through will be worth it. Soon you'll be parents and hold your tiny human in your arms.

Halftime! Give Free "New Dad" Goodwill

"Becoming a dad is not about how much you have, but how much you are willing to give. It's the most profound investment you'll ever make, with returns that last a lifetime."

— UNKNOWN

Hey dads in progress!

How's it going on this incredible journey of becoming a dad?

I hope you're enjoying the ride so far. I wanted to take a moment to check in because I know that reading "You Will Rock As a Dad!" is a bit like having a conversation with a trusted friend about the wild ride of first-time pregnancy.

By now, you've probably chuckled at the hilarious moments, nodded along with the insightful advice, and perhaps even shared a few snippets with your partner. I'm curious - how has the journey been for you halfway through the book?

I believe that your experiences and insights can be incredibly valuable for others on this adventure.

So, here's an invitation: Share your mid-book reflections with me and all other new dads-to-be!

What has stood out to you? Any "aha" moments? I'd love to hear how "You Will Rock As a Dad!" is shaping your perspective on the exciting path to fatherhood.

By sharing your thoughts, experiences, and the impact the book had on you, you provide valuable insights that can guide and reassure other dads-to-be.

I humbly request your help.

Would you be willing to share your review as it can offer a glimpse into the real-world application of the advice and tools provided in the book?

Your words have the power to inspire and equip fellow dads for the challenges and joys that lie ahead, fostering a sense of camaraderie and mutual growth in the community of first-time fathers.

So, leave a review, share your story, and let's help another first-time father out there rock as a dad.

Your gift costs 60 seconds to another new dad.

Just scan the QR code below:

Thank you for being a part of this community with me.

Let's all band together to help new dads out there navigate this exciting new life chapter.

Now, let's continue on our journey with Chapter 5.

WHAT TO EXPECT IN YOUR THIRD TRIMESTER

Women in their third trimester of pregnancy are generally highly uncomfortable. The baby's growing fast and will start to move closer to the birth canal, making it even more difficult for her to get comfortable. Imagine trying to force a watermelon through a hosepipe. This is what, in essence, will be going on inside her body. She'll struggle to do her chores around the home. Help her in any way she can. Do the laundry, clean the house, do the dishes, and make supper. The less she has to do, the more she'll be able to (at least try to) rest. She'll need all her energy for labor and childbirth.

Speaking of energy, if she gets up with the urge to clean one day, know that the end of the pregnancy is getting very close. This is called nesting and means her motherly instincts are letting her know it's time to make sure everything is ready for the baby's arrival. Many women experience this a day or two before they go into labor. If this nesting urge hits your partner, don't try and stop her. Her efforts will only cause an argument and won't get her to stop. Instead, help her as much as possible without getting in her way.

If you haven't yet gotten the baby's room ready, don't wait any longer. You'll bring your tiny human home in only a couple of weeks. Make sure everything's ready. Look at getting a changing table at a comfortable height so you and your partner won't have to bend over every time you change your baby's diaper. Look at getting a crib and a comfortable chair for feeding the baby. This will be particularly handy during nighttime feeds. You should also look for a car seat and a pram to bring the baby home safely. Decide on what you really need before you set foot in a baby store. There's a lot of equipment on the market that babies rarely use, and unless you have the financial means to splurge on items that will be used only once or twice, make sure of what you truly need. The sales staff at your local baby store will try to convince you to buy much more than you actually can afford and will use. Be strong, and don't fall for their sweet smiles and "friendly" advice. It's all just sales tactics.

Apart from being uncomfortable, she'll experience more pain leading to the end of the pregnancy. The ligaments and muscles in her tummy will be stretched to the extreme. She'll have backache(s) most days due to the extra weight she's carrying around. Her feet might get swollen, causing pain when she has to walk. The lower the baby drops into the birth canal, the more pain she'll experience in her pelvic area. Some women even describe having sharp stab-like pains in their vaginas. This is all normal. Giving her a massage can help to alleviate some of these aches, or get her heating pads. You'll seem super caring for doing this—brownie points! Otherwise, let her relax on a comfortable couch and serve her when you're at home. Even if she doesn't say or show it, she'll appreciate any help she can get.

As the pregnancy progresses, she might start to experience Braxton Hicks contractions. These are mild and irregular contractions, helping her body practice for the real deal. They are mostly just uncomfortable and can cause a slight tightness in her abdomen. The closer she gets to her due date, the more intense these practice contractions can become. Braxton Hicks causes many women to rush to the hospital, thinking they are in labor. If you know and understand the difference between Braxton Hicks and true labor, you won't only be able to calm your wife down and avoid rushing her to the hospital but also impress her with your extensive knowledge. Another partner-of-the-year award is loading!

The easiest way to determine if her contractions are Braxton Hicks or true labor is to let her walk or move. Braxton Hicks tends to go away as soon as the mom-to-be moves, whereas true labor will only stop once the baby has been born. Another way to determine what you're dealing with is to time it. True labor contractions will be regular and intensify in strength and frequency, while Braxton Hicks will be irregular and become weaker until they fade completely. Braxton Hicks will only be felt in her abdominal area, whereas true labor can be felt in the abdomen and lower back.

As the baby moves down into your wife's pelvis and becomes engaged in the birth canal, she'll become even more of a urine machine than ever before. The baby, placenta, and uterus will be pushing on her bladder, causing her to pee much more than ever before. The pressure of the dropping baby can cause your wife to swell down there, stretching her skin. Remember the two-ply toilet paper that I advised you to buy? If you haven't done that yet, now is the time. The stretched skin can quickly become sore and irritated, particularly with all the wiping from frequent toilet trips.

If you want to take your partner on one last date before the baby's arrival, be sure to take her somewhere, she'll be comfortable and won't have to walk a lot. Taking her for a meal and/or watching a movie can be a good way for her to relax. If you opt for a movie, book your tickets early enough to ensure you can get an aisle seat for her, as she'll probably have to make a couple of loo breaks during the movie. If you have a cinema close to you with recliner chairs, spend a little bit of extra money on that cinema, as these will be much more comfortable for her. When choosing a movie, keep in mind that this date is to spoil her, so choose something she'll enjoy and want to see. Research the film's running time beforehand, as you don't want to take her to watch something three hours long. Even in the most comfortable recliner chair, she'll get uncomfortable sitting for that long.

You can also look at treating her with a pedicure, either by yourself or at a salon or spa. With her growing tummy, there will be no way she'll be able to safely reach her sore feet and toes for the care she deserves. During labor, her feet will likely be on display in stirrups. Her dogs will be out! Make sure she doesn't feel ashamed of the condition of her feet. While we're on the topic of personal care, help her out by shaving her legs, and if this is what she prefers, trim or shave her vagina as well. It has likely been a couple of weeks since she was last able to see down there, and even with all the mirrors in the world, she'll struggle to clean up the downstairs area. Her vagina will be the main attraction during labor, so help her so that it's in the condition she prefers.

It's good to practice your go-to answer for questions such as "Do I look fat?" or "Is my tummy huge?" If you have answers ready for these trick questions, you can answer quickly with a smile and without hesitation. A suggested answer will be something like, "Absolutely not. You're beautiful."

Lastly, as she reaches full-term pregnancy, she might become desperate to start labor. Old wives' tales want people to believe that drinking castor oil or eating Vaseline can help to bring on labor. However, medical professionals advise against this, as it can cause serious harm to the mom-to-be and the unborn baby. She can try many safer options, such as walking, bouncing carefully on a yoga ball, or eating spicy food (best to avoid this if she's struggling with heartburn). Another option that has some scientific backing, is sex. The theories as to why this might be the preferred go-to to get labor kickstarted include:

Having an orgasm can help to stimulate the womb into starting true labor contractions.

Your semen can help to ripen the opening of her cervix. Sex, particularly nipple stimulation, triggers the release of oxytocin, the same hormone that helps bring on contractions.

Should your partner agree to try this, take your time in finding a position that will work for her, and work around the big tummy as much as possible. If she doesn't feel up to this, never put any pressure on her. She's extremely uncomfortable and a fantastic mama already growing your tiny human. Be kind to her at all times. She's exhausted.

There are, however, instances where sex will become an absolute hard no. This will be after her water breaks, if she has placenta praevia (low-lying placenta—your OB-GYN will inform you during an ultrasound scan if this is a problem), or if she has any bleeding. It's always best to discuss this with your OB-GYN to avoid your penis causing any harm to your new family member.

YOUR BABY'S DEVELOPMENT

By the time your wife reaches the third trimester of pregnancy, the baby's significant development has been completed. Their lungs are more mature but won't be able to breathe until around 36 to 38 weeks. They will, however, start to practice breathing around week 32. Since all the other major organs will be ready for your baby to survive outside the womb, your baby will now start to gain weight (and do this quickly) to make sure they have enough fat in their little bodies to keep them warm after birth.

The baby's pupils will become reactive to light, and their bones will harden. They will be able to suck their thumbs and cry. The lanugo, or layer of downy hair on their bodies, will start to disappear, and their skin will absorb the vernix caseosa, that white, creamy layer protecting their skin from the amniotic fluid. By the time they reach their due date, the average baby is 20 in. (50 cm) long and weighs about 7.5 lb (3.4 kg) (Healthdirect Australia, 2020).

Even though pregnancy is generally 40 weeks long, the baby's considered full-term from week 37 onwards. Some pregnancies last longer than 40 weeks. Generally, your OB-GYN will look at inducing labor if it has not started naturally by 42 weeks.

YOUR CHILD'S ALMOST HERE! THINK ABOUT A NAME

Naming your child will be one of the greatest decisions you'll make. It's a decision that your child will carry with them for their entire life, so carefully consider this. You might feel pressure from family members to continue the family legacy names, but ultimately, what you decide to name your child has got nothing to do with anyone but you and your partner. Let's look at some of the things you might want to consider when deciding on a name:

Forget the trends

Many people use the latest trends to decide on a name for their child. Too often, these trends pass quickly, and your child might be stuck with a name that might sound ridiculous in a couple of years. When wanting to use a trend as a name, think about how this name will sound in 10 or 20 years time. Will your child have to explain how their parents got this name daily? Will this name embarrass your child? Maybe you'll realize that naming your child born in the middle of the NFL season "Footie" might not be the best idea.

Think about the spelling

Misspelling names on purpose is another thing to carefully consider. Instead of going for the traditional "Rebecca," some opt to spell their children's names "Rabhekkha" or "Rybecka." Although there's nothing wrong with changing the spelling of your child's name, consider how often they would have to spell their names to others and how often their child's name might get mispronounced.

Consider the classics

Some names have been around for centuries, and there's a reason for that. As boring as the classics might seem, deciding on a name that has stood the test of time will ensure your child won't have to explain this name, spell it out, or have it mispronounced.

The family tree

If you decide you want to use a family name for your child, there's nothing wrong with it. However, you don't necessarily have to go for the most immediate family name. Look back at the names of your great-grandparents. There might be something golden hiding way up high in your family tree.

Look at your culture or religion

Opting to honor your culture or religion in your child's name can be a good idea. If you follow the Christian religion, there are many gems of names in the Bible, such as Noah, Luke, Hannah, and Eve. Exploring your culture and religion might just help you find the winner.

Research the meanings

Before you settle on a name, make sure it has the meaning you think it has. Many people might not know that the name "Cameron" means crooked nose. This name is of Scottish origin, and according to the native Scottish Gaelic language, *cam* is translated to "crooked," and *sròn* means "nose." It's believed that the name originated as a nickname given to a member of a Highland clan who obviously had a real looker of a nose. As much as the funny or weird meanings of names aren't always known, these hidden meanings tend to come out on the school playground. So, either make sure there are no funny hidden meanings or practice a one-liner with your child to shut up any possible mockers.

Think about nicknames

While we're on the subject of school ground mocking, consider all possible nicknames your child might have based on their names. An excellent example is Richard, who is often called "Dick." Carefully consider if this is what you want for your innocent bundle of joy. Again, if you're set on this name, help your child with appropriate comebacks to any mocking.

Look at the initials

If you decide to give your child more than one name, write out the initials of the chosen names to make sure it doesn't spell anything funky. Your child might end up being "Lily Olivia Leah" (L. O. L.), "Frederick Michael Lucas" (F. M. L.), or "Ashley Steven Shaun" (A. S. S.). Not being careful of this might scar your child for life.

To use a middle name or not

Even though you should be careful with the initials of your child's name, using a middle name can be an easy way to deal with the pressures of using a family name. Instead of naming your child, for example, Nicholas XI, use Nicholas as a second name and go wild with picking your favorite name to actually call your child.

Say it

Once you've narrowed down your choices, say the names with your last name to hear how it sounds. Your initial favorite might soon be less of a favorite. An example of this is calling your daughter Addison Jackson. It might seem like a good idea, but hearing it, you might feel like there are just too many *sons* in it. If you have family members with strange accents, also consider how your child's name will sound when they say it. This can also put a damper on your original favorite.

Do more research

It can help to do a thorough online search of your favorite names to see where they may have been associated with a villain or someone with a bad reputation. Suddenly, the name Joseph might remind you of Joseph Stalin, or naming your baby Ursula will remind you of The Little Mermaid every time you call her. There might even be a porn star using the exact same name and surname. This might also be something you want to consider avoiding.

CHOOSE A GODPARENT OR GUARDIAN

Another big decision you and your wife will have to make is deciding who to ask to be your baby's godparents or guardians. **Godparents** traditionally fill a spiritual role in your baby's life. If you're religious, they will be responsible for making sure your child is brought up understanding your religion and the higher power or God you pray to. Unless you specifically name them as your child's legal guardian in your will, they will only be there to guide your child, not to take care of your child should you and your partner be unable to.

Guardians will be the ones taking over the role of your child's parents in the event of death or incapability. As mentioned above, a guardian must be named in your will. It's always best to discuss your wishes with your chosen guardians in case of an unfortunate event. This is probably one of the most important decisions you'll make as a parent.

So, in short, your child doesn't necessarily need to have a godparent if you aren't religious or don't see the need for one, but all children should have a legal guardian specified in their parents' will. Otherwise, your child could be left in the state's care, who will then decide on an appropriate person to care for your child.

Whether you're choosing a godparent or guardian for your child, the same critical factors should be considered:

Make sure the person will be there for your child

In general, most parents choose to appoint someone who is family, as they are likely to be involved in your child's life for the long haul. Should you go for a friend, make sure you have a long, solid relationship, and should quarrels ever arise, sort any issue out as soon as possible. There's no point in having someone as your child's godparent or guardian if your child doesn't know them and they haven't been part of their life. The new buddy you might have made at the bar shortly before your wife became pregnant is probably not the ideal person to ask to play this role in your child's life.

Consider the influence they will have on your child's life

Think about the moral values of these people. Are they kind? Do they show respect to others? What will they teach your child? Do they have a similar type of lifestyle to yours? These factors are often just as important as whether they will have the financial means to care for your little one. It might sound like common sense, but these are all essential things to consider and think over with your partner.

Make sure you choose your child's godparents or guardians for the right reasons

Often a best friend or sibling will expect you to select them. However, pleasing these people might not be in your child's best interests. Instead, choose someone you trust with your life, as you will, in essence, hand over your life to them should something happen to you.

Have a frank discussion with your chosen godparents or guardians about expectations

Tell them exactly what you want them to do and what type of role you want them to play in your child's life. Similarly, they should explain their expectations as well. In the case of guardians, they might want to know what type of financial provisions you're making for your child. Play open cards with them, and should you decide to take out policies for your child, make sure the guardians have all the details of these policies and any pension funds or other savings you might have.

Never take it to heart if your chosen godparent or guardian declines the invitation. They might have personal reasons why they don't feel they should accept this responsibility. If you want, ask them to still play an important but unofficial role in your child's life. Should you decide to name either your parents or your in-laws to be the guardians, make sure to revisit this decision annually. They will get older and might become incapable of looking after a young child. So as much as they might be the ideal choice now, they might not be as suitable in a couple of years' time.

PRACTICAL NEW DAD TIP

If you want to buy new furniture for your home, carefully consider what you'll buy. Your baby might do a number on the new couch you buy, so it doesn't have to be the prettiest or whitest piece of furniture.

Wake up early on a Saturday morning before your wife pops your soon-to-be baby and go garage sale hunting. You'd be surprised how many people would practically give away their furniture to you for great bargains. Also, Craigslist has a free section where people give away all kinds of items every week. It's worth checking both of these out. And I bet your pregnant partner will be happy that you scored such a great deal.

CHAPTER SIX

YOU'RE IN DOUBLE OVERTIME

Wifey has reached the end of the pregnancy. The moment you've both been waiting and preparing for over the past nine months is getting closer by

the day. Now it's time to have your game face on and be ready for whatever can happen during this double-overtime phase.

To make sure you're ready, we'll go over every step, including what to take with you to the hospital, when to go to the hospital, what to expect in the delivery room, what will happen during a C-section if your wife will need one, and any other possibilities that can occur during the birth of your child. It's go time!

WHAT TO PACK FOR THE HOSPITAL

Once your partner starts experiencing Braxton Hicks contractions, it's good to pack the bags to take with you to the hospital, so you're ready for when the real deal comes. This will include everything your partner and baby will need during and after the birth, as well as snacks for yourself during the delivery. When getting everything together for your partner and the baby, prepare for at least a four-day stay. If the baby's born via natural vaginal birth, you'll likely bring your new family home the next day. However, if there are complications or your baby's born via a cesarean section, their hospital stay can extend to a couple of days. The average length of a hospital stay post-C-section is two to four days. Be prepared for this.

Helping a mom-to-be in labor and caring for a brand-new life will likely make you run around like a chicken with its head cut off. Don't add any more stress by not packing everything you'll need. It can be good to leave a copy of your house keys with a trusted family member or friend. This way, you can ask them to bring anything you might have forgotten to the hospital instead of driving up and down when your partner needs you the most.

To help you up your game in your new daddy role, I've included checklists of everything that should be packed for the hospital.

Also, now would be a great time to download that checklist by scanning the QR code at the start of the book. This way, you can easily check off some of those essentials that you'll need to bring to the hospital. That was a great starting checklist, however, we now need to dive into the remaining essential items to bring with you!

Mom's Bag for Delivery

This bag will contain everything your wife might need during labor. Remember that labor can easily last for numerous hours, especially with a first pregnancy.

Paperwork

Many hospitals require the mom-to-be to register and book a bed at the hospital. If that is the case, most of the paperwork will be sorted out before the delivery. Whether this is the case or not, make sure you have any necessary medical records, your wife's ID, and your health insurance card ready when you take your laboring wife to the hospital. You'll likely be expected to open her file at admissions after you take your wife to the delivery room.

Make this trip to admissions as short as possible by having all possible documents ready.

Her birth plan

We've discussed the birth plan already. You might have handed in a copy of the birth plan by the hospital beforehand. Whether this was the case or not, make sure to bring a copy with you to the hospital. If your partner's labor progresses fast, there will be no time for the hospital staff to search for her birth plan. Have it ready.

Bathrobe

The hospital will give your wife a theater gown to put on while in labor. These gowns are not exactly glamorous or comfortable. Most are open at the back. During labor, the nurses might advise your wife to walk around the ward to help her labor progress. Don't let her walk around with her bum exposed. She'll already feel like she's a part of an interactive museum exhibition by the way the nursing staff will look at her open legs and check how far her cervix has dilated using their gloved hands. Let her keep the little bit of dignity she might still have left by keeping her behind covered.

Socks

During labor, the blood flow in her body will change, with her body directing the focus toward her contracting uterus. This can result in her feet feeling cold. Pack thick socks in the bag, so she's warm and comfortable.

Slippers

Since the mom-to-be might be advised to walk around the labor ward, remember to pack slippers to reduce the risk of her slipping and hurting herself or the baby. Make sure she can put these slippers on easily by herself and that they don't fit too tightly on her swollen feet.

Lip balm

During labor and delivery, her lips might get chapped. Giving her some lip balm will bring her much-needed relief.

Face cloth

Many women feel extremely hot during delivery and will sweat profusely. Pack a face cloth to help her through this. Be the best husband by keeping this face cloth (moist and cool, of course) in hand during delivery to place on her face or forehead to cool her off.

Hair ties and clips

If your wife sweats during delivery, she might get irritated by hair hanging on her face, making her feel even hotter. In what can only be described as a superman moment, you can take out hair ties and clips and show your quick instincts by gently tying her hair back. Then, give yourself a quick pat on the back for remembering to bring these before surrendering your hand back to her (not-so-merciful) squeezes.

Entertainment

As we've said, labor can take hours. Pack some entertainment for both of you. This can be magazines or books or downloading her favorite shows or podcasts onto a device to watch. This can help distract her from what her body is going through while keeping her mind off how long labor is taking.

Her preggy pillow

The hospital will give her pillows, but these might not be the most comfortable. Try and help her by taking her preggy pillow (or favorite pillow) with you to the hospital. She might not be able to take it to the delivery room but can use it in the labor ward and after the baby's birth.

Mom's Bag for After Birth

After your wife has shown her true Wonder Woman spirit by giving birth to your baby, make sure she feels at home during the rest of her hospital stay. Remember to pack enough clothes and toiletries for at least a four-day stay.

Comfortable pajamas

Whether she gives birth naturally or via cesarean section, she'll want to feel as comfortable as possible afterward. Pack her favorite pajamas or treat her to new ones. If she plans to breastfeed, make sure the pajama top can open in the front. Opt for pajamas darker in color, so she isn't overcome with embarrassment should she fill her maternity pad so quickly that blood leaks onto her pajamas. Since babies can't generate their own body heat, the temperatures in maternity wards are typically kept quite warm. She'll also handle the baby, covered in warm blankets, often. Make sure to pack cooler pajamas for her additionally, so she doesn't get too hot.

Nursing bras

If she breastfeeds the baby, nursing bras will be a lifesaver for her. On these bras, the cups open in the front, creating easy access to release the nipple for feeds. If she opts to feed the baby formula, ensure she has comfortable bras, as she wouldn't want the girls hanging loosely when visitors come. Now isn't the time to wear lace push-up bras. Cotton bras without any underwires will likely be most comfortable.

Extra underwear

After giving birth, she'll bleed more than a year's worth of periods combined. This might cause her to leak onto her underwear. Make sure she has enough spare underwear to change regularly.

Maternity pads

Speaking of blood, she'll need maternity pads for the first couple of days after birth. These pads look more like surf-boards than regular protective products. Never mention the size of them. Just hand her one without making any type of face when she needs one. In case of severe bleeding or during the night, it can help to double-pad. Give her this tip to show you're not grossed out by it.

Breast pads and nipple cream

If she opts for breastfeeding, pack her some breast pads. This will absorb any milk leakage, so she doesn't sit with embarrassing wet marks on her pajama tops. Breastfeeding, especially at the beginning, can be extremely painful. She and her baby will learn to find the best ways for the baby to latch. This process can result in severely sore and even cracked nipples. Using a nipple cream can reduce the pain she'll experience.

Toiletries

Any toiletries she'll use on an ordinary vacation trip, she'll need in the hospital. This includes soap or shower gel, shampoo, conditioner, face wash, toothpaste, toothbrush, hairbrush, hair ties or clips, deodorant, and whatever else she might use.

Charger

Many couples forget to take phone chargers with them. Your phone's battery will deplete quickly due to all the photos taken, phone calls, and messages received. Remember to also take an extension cord in case the plug in her ward is far from her bed. An extension cord can help her use her phone while sitting comfortably on the bed.

Clothes

Even though she'll likely be in pajamas during her hospital stay, she'll need a clean set of clothes for when she's discharged, and you take her home. If she has had a C-section, make sure these clothes are comfortable and loose-fitting, as the cut on her abdomen will be sore.

Snacks and drinks

The hospital will provide her with meals, but she might want some comfort food after giving birth. Pack as many of her favorite snacks as you can fit in the bag. Remember to also pack some water or juice, especially if she's going to breastfeed, as feeding her baby can dehydrate her quickly.

Your Bag for Delivery

As we've mentioned, labor can take a good number of hours. Make sure you take everything you'll need to make it as comfortable and pleasant as possible for you.

Snacks and drinks

You'll get hungry during labor, and you don't want to have to run to a shop every time you feel like having a snack or a drink of water. Pack enough snacks for you and your wife. If your wife's doctor advises that she shouldn't eat, don't be that guy to eat in front of her, even if she says it's okay. Believe me, it's not okay. Have a bite of something while you're in the passageways on a phone call or while the doctor is busy examining your wife.

Clothes

You won't know how long you'll be in the hospital for labor, so it's always the safest option to take an extra set of clothes. You also don't know what might happen during delivery. I don't want to freak you out, but many women experience nausea and vomiting due to the extreme pain from labor. Your wife might vomit while you're still helping her to the bathroom, leaving you in the firing line. Surprisingly, being vomited on will probably not be the last time you're around an exchange of fluids that day. And, with a newborn at home, it'll definitely not be the last time someone will vomit on you. Embrace this new part of fatherhood, and change clothes as soon as your wife's safely back in bed.

Pillow

Since labor can take a good couple of hours and the chairs in the labor ward might not be the most comfortable, taking a pillow with you might be helpful. Rest while you can, especially during the beginning of labor. Once the labor intensifies, there will be no rest for either of you. Imagine an all-nighter on steroids!

Toiletries

After the baby's born and your wife's safely in the maternity ward with your newborn, you might want to freshen up quickly. Take some toiletries for yourself, even if it's just a toothbrush.

Phones, cameras, batteries, and chargers

Remember what we said about your first duty as a new father being that of a photographer or videographer? Don't forget to pack the equipment you might need. If your phone takes good photos, make sure your phone is fully charged before your partner is moved from the labor ward to the delivery room. If you're going to use a camera, pack extra batteries. You don't want to miss a single moment of what is to come.

Entertainment

Here is a *big* and *important* note: Only watch some Netflix while your wife doesn't need your help and is in the labor ward. The minute your wife moves to the delivery room, you shouldn't even touch your phone unless she wants you to record the delivery. Otherwise, pick up your phone or camera after your baby has been born to take photos.

Baby's Bag

After you've packed all the other bags, it's now time to think about what your baby will need. Now is also a good time to make sure the baby's car seat is installed in your car. Practice exactly how to use it. This might sound ridiculous; how hard can it be to click the clips in right? Well, you'd be surprised just how much you might struggle with this seemingly simple task when you have to secure a crying baby in it for the first time.

Clothes

Take enough clothes for the baby to wear for at least four days. Work on about two outfits per day, as you'll have to change your baby's clothes more often in case of spit-ups. Even though some super cute outfits are available in the shops, pack something comfortable instead. Soft onesies are always a good option.

Socks and beanies

As we've mentioned, newborns can't generate their own body heat due to their limited body fat and their little body's inability to metabolize the fat. They also can't shiver, a way in which a person can increase body heat. Make sure your baby will be warm enough. Even if your baby's onesie covers their feet, put a pair of socks on their tiny feet underneath the outfit. Babies lose a lot of their body heat through their heads, so pack at least one beanie to wear daily.

Blankets

Take some receiving and warm blankets. Receiving blankets are great to use to swaddle a baby. Warm blankets can be great when you do skin-to-skin contact since your baby will only wear a diaper, and you won't have your shirt on during this time. Make sure you both stay warm.

Diapers

Some hospitals will provide diapers for your baby's stay, while others request you to bring them. Make sure to find out the policy for the hospital your partner will be giving birth. If ever in doubt, pack a couple of diapers in the bag, and leave more in the car or with someone you know will be there as soon as visitors are allowed.

Wet wipes

The same goes for wet wipes. Some hospitals will provide them, while others expect you to bring enough for your stay. If you need to take your own supply, don't think one packet will be enough. Especially while the baby's passing meconium, the baby's first dark and extremely sticky poos. You might use a whole box of wipes on a single diaper change.

Creams

Here's a good tip to impress your wife with about meconium. Put some petroleum jelly on your baby's bum after every diaper change. The meconium will then stick to the Vaseline, not your baby's skin, making these diapers extremely easy and quick to change. Otherwise, remember to pack some bum cream to protect your baby's sensitive skin.

Toiletries

If you need to take toiletries for your baby, remember to pack body wash, body lotion, cotton balls, and surgical spirits or rubbing alcohol for cleaning the umbilical cord. Make sure all the toiletries you get for your baby are for sensitive skin. Many newborns' skins struggle with heavily fragranced products.

Burp cloth

Make sure your partner has a burp cloth ready every time she feeds or burps the baby. This can help to prevent milk spills on your clothes. We will discuss this in more detail in Chapter 8.

Pacifiers

If you decide to use a pacifier for your baby, make sure to pack that, as well as a small microwave sterilizer to clean them at the hospital. There are many benefits to using a pacifier, such as soothing a crying baby and preventing sudden infant death syndrome.

WHEN TO GO TO THE HOSPITAL

It's important to know when it's time to rush your wife to the hospital when she's in labor. We've discussed the difference between Braxton Hicks contractions and true labor, so you should be able to tell when actual labor is starting. However, contractions can continue for a good couple of hours before active labor starts. The longer you can keep your partner comfortable at home, the easier the process will be for both of you.

Your wife's OB-GYN will advise you when you must go to the hospital, and many follow the popular 5-1-1 rule. According to this, you should head to the hospital once your wife's contractions are five minutes apart, last for one minute, and continue for one hour. Keep in mind that your wife's individual case might cause your OB-GYN to advise differently, so always follow the doctor's advice.

If your wife experiences any signs of actual labor starting before she reaches 37 weeks, or if she has any vaginal bleeding, extreme dizziness, or blurred vision, take her to the hospital immediately. These can all be signs of complications, and your OB-GYN will need to examine and possibly treat your wife.

Premature Birth

If your baby's born before 37 weeks of pregnancy, it'll be classified as premature birth. It's divided into four categories (Mayo Clinic, 2021):

- **Late preterm** is when the baby's born between 34 and 36 weeks of pregnancy.
- **Moderately preterm** is when the baby's born between 32 and 34 weeks of pregnancy.
- **Very preterm** is when the baby's born earlier than 32 weeks of pregnancy.

- **Extreme preterm** is when the baby's born earlier than 25 weeks of pregnancy.

These babies can have an increased risk of medical and developmental issues, and since some of the major organs, particularly their lungs, won't be fully developed yet, they will likely spend at least a couple of weeks in the neonatal intensive care unit (NICU) at the hospital.

Apart from breathing difficulties, your baby might need help with feeding, as they may not have developed the ability to suck or swallow yet. This will then be done by inserting a feeding tube through their noses. The baby's gastrointestinal system might not have matured yet, which can lead to conditions such as necrotizing enterocolitis, where the lining of the bowel wall is injured. As scary as this can be, trust your baby's doctors. As parents, there isn't much you can do to relieve any swelling or discomfort your baby might experience.

Babies born prematurely also have an increased risk of suffering from anemia, jaundice, immune disorders, bleeding in the brain (intraventricular hemorrhage), and heart conditions such as patent ductus arteriosus, where there's an opening between the pulmonary artery and aorta.

Premature birth can lead to serious long-term complications, including cerebral palsy, problems with learning, hearing and vision issues, chronic health problems, and behavioral and psychological difficulties.

As much as it's good to take note of the problems that can arise from premature birth, don't dwell too much on this. Should your wife go into premature labor, your OB-GYN will do everything possible to stop the labor. If these steps are unsuccessful and your baby's born prematurely, specialists such as neonatologists and pediatricians will care for your little one and try to reduce any risk of serious complications. Increasing your knowledge of all the possibilities of what might happen will give you the confidence to deal with these potential situations.

LET'S TALK ABOUT BIRTH

Contractions are one of the most obvious signs of labor, but there are many other signs of labor starting that you can look out for. One of the first signs is a change in vaginal discharge, followed by a mucus plug or bloody show. This can be a pinkish or even brown jelly-like discharge, indicating the opening of her cervix. This doesn't necessarily mean labor is starting but normally indicates that labor is usually a couple of days away. Don't freak out when your wife shows you her bloody show. It'll likely not put you off eating Jell-O forever.

She might suddenly get the urge to go to the bathroom. This is caused by the baby's head pushing on her bowels. Without going into too much information here, having good bowel movements early on in labor can help your wife feel a lot more comfortable during labor. When she gets to the point of pushing the baby out, she pushes in the same way she would normally during a bowel movement. This often causes the pregnant woman to poop on the delivery table. If this happens to your wife, she might be embarrassed afterward. Don't make a big deal of it. Your OB-GYN or the nursing staff will quickly wipe the poo away. This is normal. If the doctor or nurse can deal with it without making a face, so can you.

An obvious sign that she's in labor will be when your partner's water breaks. This happens when the amniotic sac breaks, and amniotic fluid leaks out through her vagina. There's usually not much doubt when your wife's water breaks. However, don't ever wait for her water to break if her contractions meet the 5-1-1 rule. In many cases, the amniotic sac doesn't break naturally, and your OB-GYN will have to break it using a long plastic hook. Should this happen to your wife, stay calm. It shouldn't be painful for her; even if it is, it'll be nothing compared to the contractions she's experiencing. Once your partner's water breaks, your baby will most likely have to be delivered within 24 hours.

CAN YOU BE IN THE DELIVERY ROOM?

If you've ever wondered whether you should be in the delivery room for your baby's birth, stop having those thoughts right now. Your wife will need you there, even if it's just to calm her or so she can have a hand to squash during delivery. You'll also not want to miss your baby being born. However, some women do prefer their partners not to be there. Have a conversation with your wife about this beforehand, so you'll both know what the expectations are.

There are some general guidelines to be aware of the minute you step into the delivery room. The main reason you're there is to support your partner. Yes, you also want to experience your baby's birth. You'll be the least important person in the room. This is about your wife and the baby.

In the same way, as it's good to find out if your partner wants you in the delivery room, it can be helpful to discuss expectations before your wife goes into labor. Find out if she wants you to take photos or videos during delivery. Maybe all she wants is for you to hold her hand or help her with deep breathing. Either way, you'll earn some brownie points by being considerate enough to ask.

Keep your own limitations in mind when discussing these expectations. If you easily get queasy or squeamish by the sight of blood, don't volunteer to be front and center. Tell your wife you'd prefer to stand by her head and support her from there. Don't force yourself to do something you're not comfortable with.

Whatever you do, be the support she needs. Also, be aware that she might not be in a position to tell you what you can do to help her. If you took childbirth classes, try the tips given there. Otherwise, try different things to help her. Unless her doctor advises against it, you can offer her ice chips. You might think giving her a back rub will help her to deal with the pain. Yes, this might help, or it might not. If your wife screams at you to stop, then stop, smile, and try something else. Remember, she's birthing a child right now, so maybe give her space and grace to yell. Just support her! She's dealing with a lot of pain, so try anything. Trying is better than standing around being in the way. Chances are, if you do nothing to help, you'll also get shouted at. So, rather do something than nothing.

Despite what you might feel at the moment, wondering what you can do to help her is the easy part of the job. Labor is anything but easy. Regardless of how difficult it can be seeing your wife in severe pain and not knowing what to do to help her, her job of delivering the baby's a lot more difficult. Guys, you might feel like you'll die while you have the man flu. Believe me, man-flu is nothing like childbirth. Many medical professionals compare the pain from labor to breaking 20 bones in your body simultaneously. It isn't a pain you can truly explain to others. And it'll just get worse and worse until the minute the baby's shoulders are out. Be her advocate and make sure all her needs are met. This will help her focus only on giving birth without worrying about anything else.

Never focus on the clock in the delivery room. As much as it's essential to time her contractions before going to the hospital, you should forget any reference to time once you're there. The nursing staff will make sure the labor progresses. If your partner ever asks you how long the labor has been, try to be as vague as possible. Knowing that she has been at it for 19 hours won't motivate her or put her in a positive mindset. Instead, answer her something like this, "It's been a while, but we're getting there."

Always stay calm. You might see things that you wish you could unsee. Man up. It's part of this process. Never ever say anything is "gross" or 'disgusting." Don't react negatively when the family drives you insane by asking for updates. They are just as excited as you about adding this little human to the family. It can be helpful to create a group chat to add everyone who might want an update. Better yet, set the group so you can only send a message to it. And then, put your phone on silent if you still receive too many requests for updates. Your calmness will make her calmer.

This ties in with the next important point: Don't spend unnecessary time on your phone once you're in the delivery room. Make sure you show her that you're connected, committed, and with her every step of the way.

When she's crying or cursing from pain, don't tell her anything along the lines of, "It can't be that bad." Fellas, it is that bad and worse. Also, never compare it to any pain you ever might have had. That time you bumped your pinkie toe against the leg of the coffee table was nothing compared to what she's going through. Just hold her hand (or rather, allow her to squash the life out of it) or her leg, and if you have to talk, tell her how great she's doing or how proud of her you are.

Lastly, don't become a backseat pusher when it's time to push this new life out. The OB-GYN, midwife, or nurse will tell your wife what to do when to push, and when not to push. If you also get involved, it can become like a sporting event, with your yelling "push" getting louder and louder. Rather stay quiet, let her squeeze the life out of your hand, and encourage her in a low and calm tone when necessary.

PAIN MANAGEMENT DURING LABOR

Pain management should be discussed with your OB-GYN in the weeks leading up to labor. Many women opt to go for non-medical pain relief options, with many changing their minds mid-labor when the true effects of contractions can be felt. It often happens that when the mom-to-be changes her mind, her labor can have progressed too far, and she'll have no other option but to (literally!) push through. This is why it's important to know all her options before going into labor.

Let's first discuss the non-medical methods of relieving labor pains:

Antenatal or birthing classes

These can help a pregnant woman know what to expect, reducing the anxiety of childbirth. Many medical professionals argue that if you know what to expect, you can deal with pain and other uncomfortableness easier. Another way to reduce her anxiety and, as a result, help her deal with the pain is to have her partner (yes, that's you!) with her to support her.

Being fit and healthy

This is another way that can help a woman deal with labor, as she will generally have more energy and endurance. This is why it's so important to moderate exercise for as long as possible during pregnancy.

Deep breathing techniques

Many methods are known to help women get through contractions. Your wife will learn these techniques during birthing classes. Your OB-GYN, midwife, or nurse will also help your wife with her breathing during labor.

Using music

This can be a welcoming distraction that can help her deal with the pain of labor, but if she's against this, please turn it off immediately. Jamming to "Gangnam Style" might not be her cup of tea right now.

A massage

This can look like using oil, hot or cold packs, and a warm shower. If there's a handheld shower-head, she can use this to apply hot water straight to her tummy or lower back. Should she decide to shower during labor, prioritize staying close to the bathroom in case she needs help. Although these natural techniques can help, many women don't find them effective enough to relieve their labor pain. Although other medical methods can be used to reduce the feeling of pain, the following are the most popular choices used worldwide:

Nitrous oxide

If you've ever seen a pregnant woman in a movie yell, "Give me the gas!" this is what she was referring to. This gas is administered through a face mask whenever she has a contraction. This method doesn't take the pain away but takes the edge off and distracts the laboring woman as she's concentrating on inhaling the gas.

Nitrous oxide doesn't affect the baby but can cause possible mild side effects for the mom-to-be, including nausea and vomiting, confusion, and disorientation.

Pethidine

This pain reliever is in a similar class as morphine and is administered by injection. Its impact can last up to four hours and can effectively relieve labor pains. Possible side effects for mom include nausea and vomiting, disorientation, and slower breathing. It can also affect the unborn baby's breathing and ability to suck after birth. If this is the case, your doctor will administer a reversal drug for your baby. In most cases, however, the effects of the pethidine will have worked out before your baby's born.

Epidural

This is the most effective form of pain relief during labor. An anesthetic is injected into the mom-to-be's spinal cord, making her feel numb from the waist down. After getting an epidural, the OB-GYN will monitor the unborn baby's heart rate closely to make sure the baby doesn't go into fetal distress. Possible side effects include feeling faint and nauseated. A urinary catheter will have to be inserted, as she will have no bladder control, headaches, and muscle weakness in the legs, which can last for an hour or more after your baby's born. It can also affect the pregnant woman's ability to push during labor, resulting in a vacuum cup or forceps being used to deliver the baby.

WHAT'S A C-SECTION?

Complications can arise that will make a vaginal birth either too dangerous or even impossible. Usually, this will be called weeks ahead of time, but something can also happen during vaginal delivery, causing the OB-GYN to change the birthing plan. In cases like this, a C-section will be done to surgically remove the baby from the pregnant woman's uterus.

If this does happen to your wife, don't stress or freak out. About 30% of all babies in the United States are born via C-section (WebMD, n.d.). This form of birth is generally perfectly safe for both mom and baby, but since it's a major surgery where the doctor will cut through many layers of ligaments and muscles in the mom's tummy, it can make caring for the newborn more difficult. Your partner will have post-operative pain and won't be able to bend down or pick up anything heavy. Time to show your new daddy superpowers!

An epidural or spinal block will be administered before the operation, numbing the pregnant woman from the waist down. This means she'll be awake during the surgery and can see her baby minutes, if not seconds, after the baby's removed from the uterus. A screen is placed between the woman's head and body to ensure she can't see the actual operation. Without serious complications, the dad-to-be can be in the operating room during this procedure. You'll sit by your wife's head. Again, if you're squeamish at all, look at her face and not the operation. You don't want to cause a commotion by fainting midway through the birth of your baby. The whole procedure only takes between 30 to 45 minutes.

Many complications can make a C-section the safest form of delivery. If the following happens, your OB-GYN will likely perform a planned C-section:

- the baby being breech (feet to the bottom, head up) or traverse (sideways)
- the baby has congenital disabilities detected on an ultrasound scan, such as hydrocephalus the baby's too big to fit through the birth canal placenta previa (when the placenta is very low in the uterus or covers the cervix) multiple births
- the mother had a previous C-section or any form of operation on her uterus

As we've mentioned, a C-section can be performed if complications arise during labor:

- labor stops midway through
- the baby's in fetal distress
- placenta abruption (when the placenta separates from the uterine wall)
- the umbilical cord is tight around the baby's neck
- the umbilical cord enters the birth canal before the baby

There you go... You just learned a lot of information to impress your wife (and possibly even your OB-GYN). You'll now not only be able to reassure your wife with the statistics on how common C-sections are but will even be able to list the reasons for needing a C-section. You'll be able to stay calm and keep your partner calm. Brownie points are coming your way!

CHECKING BABY'S HEALTH

Shortly after your baby's born, a doctor will examine your little one. If the baby's born full-term, the specialist will be called a pediatrician. Should your baby be preterm, a neonatologist or a pediatrician will look after your baby's health.

If the delivery takes place via a C-section, this specialist will be in the operating room from the beginning of the procedure. This is because C-section babies often struggle to start breathing, as their breathing isn't stimulated to start naturally by moving through the birth canal. If this is the case with your baby, the pediatrician will replicate this stimulation to get the breathing going. If this happens, don't freak out. Pediatricians are trained to do this and probably help hundreds (if not more) of babies every year to start breathing. Stand by your wife, act as if everything is going perfectly, and wait for those first cries.

The sound of your baby's first cries might surprise you. It doesn't sound anything like the overwhelming cry you might get used to in just a couple of weeks. Those first cries actually sound more like a cat crying than a tiny human. Take this in, or better yet, make a video of your newborn's cat cries. Within only a couple of hours, this will be gone, and the crying will sound normal—a sound you'll get used to over the next couple of months.

The doctor or nursing staff will also perform two Apgar tests on your baby. This is a quick, non-invasive test done first a minute after birth to evaluate how the baby handled the birthing process and again after five minutes, to assess how the baby's coping after birth. On rare occasions, this test may be repeated again after 10 minutes. This test looks at five aspects: color, heart rate, reflexes, muscle tone, and breathing. A score of either zero, one, or two is given for each element, making up a score out of ten. The higher the score, the better your baby's coping.

PRACTICAL NEW DAD TIP

Discuss getting help before your child comes. Knowing who you have in your corner to support you during this new chapter is a great way to have peace of mind. Whether that is family helping out, friends, or hired help, it's great to have the discussion so you're aware of what you have available in any situation you might find yourself in. You might also need someone to fetch things from home that you've either forgotten or didn't think of packing. The saying goes, "It takes a village to raise a child" (Dubner, 2011). Find your village and accept their offers of help.

CHAPTER SEVEN

NATIONAL CHAMPION

You now have the most treasured prize of all! You and your partner have brought a child into this world.

Congratulations! This is even better than being a state champion. In fact, you've created your own little national champion!

You've now reached what many people call the fourth trimester of pregnancy. Your baby has been born, but now it's time to step up your dad game. Your life has changed forever for the better. Having a newborn in the home can be challenging, and many dads would prefer to fast forward through the coming months to when their child is old enough to interact and kick a ball with them. Don't be *that* dad. As much as you can look forward to having your own homegrown teammate, enjoy these coming months (even though it can be exhausting) and bond with your little one as much as you can.

YOU HAVE A CHILD, NOW WHAT?

After you've fulfilled one of your first duties of taking as many photos as possible and ensuring your wife settles into the maternity ward and gets some bonding time, it's now time for you to become a gatekeeper. The minute you let people know you're officially a dad, they will likely ask what time the hospital's visiting hours are or even just rock up there unannounced.

Your partner might be exhausted after delivery, and as much as she's looking forward to showing off your bundle of joy, both of you need to have a couple of moments to reflect on what happened, take it all in, and spend time with the baby. Your job is to support your wife and make sure she's as comfortable as possible.

If you don't feel up to having visitors yet, don't be afraid to tell them that you'll let them know when they can visit. If they arrive at the hospital uninvited, explain to them that you need time alone with the baby or that your wife is too tired. They will probably be so excited to see the baby that they won't mind waiting at the hospital's coffee shop or coming back later once all three of you are ready for people.

Once you start letting in visitors, confirm they wash their hands thoroughly as they enter the room. If anyone is sick— even the slightest sniffs—ask them to rather stay outside. Your baby will still need to build its little immune system, and the last thing you want is for your newborn to get sick (although this happens more often than you might realize). Never let anyone kiss your baby on the mouth or even on the hands. Remember, babies often put their hands in their mouths when they get hungry.

The hospital's visitation policy will likely stipulate this but never allow too many visitors simultaneously. Apart from potentially exposing your baby to germs, your little one can also get overstimulated by all the different faces, voices, and smells, and their bodies can get sore from being held like that. Protect your baby better than you would an NFL Super Bowl ring.

BREASTFEEDING

Most medical professionals will encourage your partner to breastfeed your baby. Breastmilk holds numerous benefits for the baby: It's filled with the vitamins and minerals your baby will need, is highly nutritious, offers protection against some infections, and can reduce the risk of sudden infant death syndrome, the unexplained death of a baby younger than one-year-old.

Depending on how she gave birth, the nurses will put the baby on her breast as soon as possible after birth, usually within only a few minutes. This first attempt is often unsuccessful, as your wife and baby will still be recovering from the beautiful trauma they just experienced. Babies generally don't need to feed for about an hour after birth, so if the first time doesn't work, she can try nursing again later. The nursing staff will help your wife and baby get the perfect latch. If there are problems, they will check your baby's blood sugar regularly to assess that it doesn't drop too low due to not getting any (or enough) milk. If this does happen, they will give the baby little bits of formula (often using a cup to not cause any nipple confusion) to take the edge off their hunger. If your wife continues to struggle, consider arranging a consultation with a lactation specialist in your area. The staff at the maternity ward, OB-GYN, or pediatrician will be able to recommend one. Alternatively, a quick online search will give you a list of specialists to consider.

Newborn babies must feed every two to three hours, give or take. For at least the first six weeks, or until the pediatrician gives the okay, it's important to wake your baby up for feeds. If they skip a feed, their blood sugar can drop very quickly to dangerously low levels. If your baby wants to feed more frequently than that, don't starve them. Feed them on demand when they are hungry. Apart from crying, signs that a newborn wants to feed include the following:

- Smacking their lips.
- Sticking their tongues out.
- Searching with their heads for a nipple (especially when you hold them close to you). Sucking their hands.

Since your partner will spend more than half a day breastfeeding your baby, it can be exhausting. Your wife will appreciate every bit of help, no matter how small it may seem. Be an extra set of hands for her. Your partner will need this, as breastfeeding will take over her entire life for a bit. Help her clean the breast pump's different parts after each use, or get an extra golden star by baking her lactation cookies to snack on. Many recipes are available online and are so easy to make that they are relatively foolproof.

Even though you won't be able to physically help with the middle of-the-night feeds, there are many ways you can make these feeds easier on her. Get up to change the diaper, or burp the baby once the feed is done. This way, your wife can get some more rest. If you're afraid to burp the baby or don't know how to do this (after all, your burps come out naturally by themselves), don't fret, we'll discuss this and give helpful tips in Chapter 8.

Apart from supporting her with logistics, be there for her emotionally. Many women can't breastfeed. This can be due to having inverted nipples or insufficient glandular breast tissue to produce sufficient milk. Others have to stop due to allergies or illness. This can wreak a mama emotionally, making her feel like the worst mother for not being able to feed her baby. Be a rock for your wife. Remind her to stop feeling guilty. There are brilliant formulas on the market.

In the end, the only thing that truly matters is that your baby's fed.

Choose the method—breastfeeding, expressing (when mom pumps and provides the breast milk with a bottle), or using formula—that fits into your life. In a couple of years, your child will likely eat old French fries off a dirty carpet in the car, so ultimately, whether a child is breast- or bottle-fed isn't a life-or-death decision. Just make sure your baby isn't hungry.

If she does breastfeed, remember that mama's breasts are now holding your baby's food. Should your wife allow you some playtime there and you do get a mouthful of milk, don't freak out. Swallow it as quickly as possible without mentioning it or spit it out. Remember that if you make a big deal out of it, you might not be allowed close to them again, so choose your best option carefully (I've learned this the hard way).

YOUR FAMILY IS HOME

Just as you and your partner seem to settle into your roles as parents (with the help of the nursing staff, of course), you hear the most surprisingly frightening words: Mom and baby have been discharged. It's now time to put on your big boy undies. You're about to take an actual living baby home. You and your partner will be solely responsible for keeping your baby alive. If a profanity or two slips out, no one will blame you. This can be scary. Remember the tip on practicing how to use the baby seat for the car? You're probably thanking me right about now...

Once you're home, take as much off her plate as possible. She'll be exhausted, and her body will need time to recover. If you have time off from work (paternity leave), let her rest as much as possible. Look after your baby (especially during the first two weeks they will sleep most of the time), do the laundry, wash the dishes, clean the house, and cook food. Some of your loved ones might offer to bring meals. Even if you don't like a specific aunt's cooking, accept it with a smile. It's one less thing for you and your partner to worry about.

You might notice your newborn's skin gets a yellowish tinge after a few days. This is jaundice and is a surprisingly common occurrence in newborns. The best home remedy for this is to expose the baby's skin (through a window or lace curtain) to sunlight daily. Use this as an excuse to relax and bond with the baby. Sit in a comfy chair, and let your baby sleep on your chest. If you want to be a super dad, remove your shirt and combine it with skin-to-skin contact. You will be a miracle jaundice healer, your wife will also have some time to relax, and your baby (and you) can have the first of many naps together.

While we're on the subject of skin-to-skin contact, you might wonder what the big deal of doing this is and even how to do this. Let's get into the how first: You simply take off your shirt, take off the baby's clothes (but keep the diaper on!), and sit comfortably on a chair while you let your baby lay tummy down on your bare chest. Remember to cover your baby's back with a blanket to stay warm. Doing this holds endless benefits for your baby. Amongst others, it helps regulate your baby's heart rate and breathing, reduces the cortisol levels of both you and the baby, and provides a great bonding opportunity.

Another way to bond with your baby and help your wife is to take care of bath time. No boobs are needed to bathe a baby, so this is a sure way dad can help. Before they are discharged from the hospital, a nurse will likely give your baby their first bath. Go with them for this bath and take note of what the nurse is doing. If you follow these steps, bath time is easy. In fact, as long as you try your best to not get water in your baby's ears or let them drown, you can't go wrong here.

You might find yourself freaking out about nothing. If your baby sneezes, it might feel to you like they have pneumonia. You're not a hypochondriac. You're a new parent who wants the best for their little human. If you ever feel unsure, call your baby's pediatrician for advice. Remember, something that doesn't seem very serious with an infant can become life-threatening in a matter of hours. You'd rather call them unnecessarily than ignore something that could potentially be a serious concern. If any of the following happens, you should definitely make the call or take the baby to see the doctor (Ben-Joseph, 2018):

- rectal temperature of 100.4 °F (38 °C) in babies younger than two months
- bloody vomit or poo
- more than eight runny poos in eight hours (yes, your baby's poo won't only be of huge interest to you but also become a topic of conversation)
- fontanelle (soft spot on your baby's head) bulging out
- fast breathing, particularly if your baby turns blue around the mouth
- difficulty waking your baby up signs of dehydration
- sunken eyes
- no wet diapers for six hours crying without tears
- fontanelle sinking in

YOUR LIFE HAS CHANGED

If your work permits time off as paternity leave, take it. Even if you don't feel like you need it, it's essential to spend this time at home, bonding with your baby and helping your partner adjust to her new role as a mom... and yours as a first-time dad!

You'll both be sleep-deprived, and chances are this will continue for at least a couple of weeks. On top of this, you'll be nervous about ensuring your newborn's needs are met and may also feel anxious about this journey.

While your wife and baby will be your top priorities, it's crucial that you still make time for yourself. Make time to do something you enjoy, even if it's just a quick stop at the gym on the way home from work or reading an extra comic book while sitting on the toilet. Give your wife the same opportunity to do something by herself. If she's breastfeeding, this will have to be between feeds. Make sure you're there for her.

Self-care is vital in this new phase of your life. If you deplete all your energy, it'll have a significant impact on your new family. Do what you need to do to make sure you stay sane. Look out for any signs of postpartum depression in yourself and your partner. Support each other and, if need be, seek professional help. Your baby needs their parents mentally strong to take care of them.

PRACTICAL NEW DAD TIP

Wet wipes are the Swiss Army knife for babies and toddlers. Have extra sets of baby wipes in all places of your home and living space. Place them in the living room, bedroom, kitchen, backyard, and car, and make sure there are always tons of wipes in the diaper bag. You never know when you'll need them. Your partner will forever be grateful for planning ahead.

CHAPTER EIGHT

TIME TO BE A DAD

Now that you're a father and have brought your brand new family member home, it's time for you to be a dad. You've made it through the pregnancy, you (and your partner) have survived the birth, your hand has recovered from being squeezed during labor, and all three of you have settled back home.

The worst part is over. However, you might still feel unsure about how to care for your baby. As fragile as they look (and are), they don't break easily. Get those fears of picking your tiny human up out of your mind. Otherwise, you'll never get to bond with your little one or help your wife with parenting duties.

Let's get the first thing out of the way. When you're looking after your child, never call it babysitting. A babysitter is someone you pay to look after your child when you're not available. Unless you're getting paid for looking after your child, you're not babysitting. You're parenting and being a father, not just a sperm donor who helped to create the baby and can now sit back and relax.

YOU'RE OFFICIALLY A PARENT

Being a dad doesn't mean you'll chill on the couch while your wife does all the nursing, caring, and bonding. Being a dad means being involved, from changing those soiled diapers to burping your baby and calming them when they cry.

Don't run for the hills now. As overwhelming as this might sound, being a dad will soon be second nature, especially if you use these handy tips.

Handling Your Baby

Always supporting the baby's neck is the most important thing to remember when handling and holding your newborn. Very young babies have weak neck muscles and can't hold their heads (which might seem way too big for their little bodies) up by themselves. If you pick a young baby up without supporting their neck, you might cause their head to dangle or flop, which could cause not only damage to their fragile neck but also severe brain injury. When you pick your new baby up, always place one hand under the baby's neck and support the lower back or bum with your other hand or arm. As long as you do this, your baby will be fine. You can do this! At first, you might concentrate that your hands are in the right place, but after doing this a couple of times, it'll feel completely natural. You'll even be able to do this half-asleep during a night-time feed.

Continue supporting your baby's neck until its muscles are strong enough to hold its head up by themselves. This usually happens between three to six months. Don't "test" the strength of your baby's neck by removing the support. Instead, keep an eye on your baby when they are enjoying tummy time or lying down. Once you see them lifting their heads by themselves, you'll know you can start to slowly reduce the support.

Change a Diaper

Changing a baby's diaper is probably one of the worst jobs as a parent, but if you want a happy marriage, don't expect your wife to do this task alone. Mentally prepare yourself for this, as you'll do this often because babies can be pooping machines. It's easy to determine if your baby needs a change. If the diaper is filled with wee, it'll feel full and heavy, while you'll be able to smell a poop diaper, sometimes a mile away.

If you do get the whiff, make sure you have plenty of wet wipes close to you before you start removing the baby's clothes. Alternatively, get the bath water ready. Babies can leave waste explosions at times that won't only need almost a whole packet of wipes to clean, but a bath might also be necessary to make sure no excess poop is left on the skin. The acidity in their poop can irritate or burn a baby's sensitive skin very quickly.

To determine the level of hazard you're dealing with, you can gently pull the diaper away from the baby's back or thigh and have a quick peek. This can also help you determine whether you should grab a gas mask to protect yourself from the violent smell that can feel like a bullet to the head once it hits you.

Once you know what you're dealing with, get all the necessary equipment ready. Apart from the gas mask, bath water, and wipes, this will also include a clean diaper, bum cream to protect the sensitive skin against irritation by the excretions, and sometimes even a clean set of clothes in the case of a severe explosion.

If you have a boy, always put a wet wipe, face cloth, or another sort of cover over the penis during diaper changes. If not, you risk getting hit in the face by a tiny pee fountain. Also, point the penis down when putting on a new diaper. Otherwise, you'll end up changing your little peeing machine's clothes more often than his diapers.

When putting on a new diaper, always remember the side with the sticky tabs on is the back. The sticky tabs fasten on the front of the diaper. You should secure the diaper enough to stay in position but never too tight. You can do a quick finger test to determine if it's too tight: If you can slide your finger between your baby's skin and diaper with relative ease, it should be fine. Once you're done and the baby's clothed, pat yourself on the back.

Burp Your Baby

In the first three months of a baby's life, it's important to burp them after every feed, sometimes even in the middle of one. This is because babies swallow a lot of air bubbles as they drink, which will cause discomfort for the baby afterward. Imagine yourself downing a gallon of beer and the discomfort the gassiness will cause. This is similar to what a baby feels. Only their little bodies can't burp (or sometimes even fart) by themselves.

There are many ways to burp a baby. One of the most common methods is to let your baby sit on your lap and support their neck by placing one hand under their chin. Gently rub your baby's back, bottom to top, repeatedly. You can also bounce your leg, but make sure these are minimal movements. You don't want to shake your baby doing this. You can also let your baby lie stomach down over your lap, with their belly resting on your thigh, or hold your baby against your chest with their chin resting on your shoulder. Rub your baby's back from the bottom to the top, or pat your baby's back gently.

Make sure you always have a burp cloth ready, as a baby often spits up a bit of milk as they burp. Let me give you a little warning: Don't wear your newest work shirt when doing this. These gentle burps can sometimes turn into projectile vomiting, which can not only stain your shirt but leave you smelling just as sour as your mood might be.

CALM YOUR CRYING, BABY

Knowing how to comfort your baby when they cry can go a long way in preserving your sanity. Some babies cry more than others, seemingly for no reason whatsoever. If this is the case for you, the word "colic" will probably start feeling like profanity. Colic happens when your crying machine revs up at specific times of the day, sometimes for hours at a time, with no apparent reason or cause for the crying.

Unfortunately, no matter how healthy the mom's pregnancy is or how smoothly the birth goes, there's no way to know if your baby will be crabby or happy. It's the luck of the draw. If your baby does have colic, this usually subsides after three to six months. During this time, remember those grandmas, grandpas, aunts, and uncles who will be eager to look after your scream machine while you and your wife recharge outside the house.

If you want to be a super dad in a happy marriage, here is a checklist of what you can look out for when your baby cries:

Diaper

Do a quick smell and feel test. You'd also cry if you pooped your pants and were left to lay in the poop. Remember, the diaper doesn't have to be soiled to bother your baby. A soggy diaper is heavy and restricts a baby's movement.

Hungry

If it's almost time for a feed, get the bottle ready or hand the baby over to mom for some boob recharge. While your wife's breastfeeding your baby, pretend you need to do something urgently outside and go catch a breath of fresh air to decompress. Remember, it's important to take care of yourself too. I don't intend to sound like a broken record, but taking care of you is necessary. Then, rush back to burp the baby or catch and clean any projectile vomit.

Tired or overstimulated

Small babies are supposed to sleep most of the day. If the *crank o' meter* shoots up after your baby has been awake for a while, it might be tired or overstimulated. Keep in mind that your baby had little to no excitement in the womb, so seeing the world might get a bit much for them. Take them to a quiet room to relax and fall asleep.

Too hot or cold

Young babies can't regulate their body heat yet, so you'll always need to dress them correctly. The general rule of thumb is to dress your baby in one more layer than you're wearing.

Gas

If your crying machine revs up shortly after a feed, try to burp your baby again. If burping doesn't help, your baby might struggle to fart (yes, that does happen). Lay them on their back and move their legs up and down like they are riding a bicycle, or massage their stomach in a clockwise, circular movement.

Lonely

If your baby wakes up screaming alone in the crib in the room, they might want someone to hold them and make them feel safe and secure. Get your bonding going by cuddling with your little one.

Sick

Unfortunately, babies are born with no immune system to protect them from germs, so they get sick easily. Do yourself a favor and invest in a forehead thermometer. Check their temperatures if you find no other source for the extra crabbiness. If that seems fine, see if their noses are congested or gently push on the tragus (the triangular piece of ear covering the opening) of their ears. If your baby has an earache, their crying will turn to screaming from touching the ear. Now you know it's time to visit the doctor. If their noses are congested, you use a couple of drops of saline nasal spray or breastmilk to loosen the snot. Also, consider investing in a little device you use to suck the snot from your baby's nose. It sounds disgusting, but trust me, the relief your baby will experience will make life much more pleasant for everyone around. And these devices do have little sponges in to make sure no snot will get to your mouth while sucking. It'll be fine!

If you've ticked everything on your checklist and your baby's still a cranky pant, don't lose hope. Try the following five things before you order noise-canceling earphones:

Pacifier

Not all babies like to suckle on a pacifier, but it can do wonders to keep the crying machine quiet. Some people are against the use of a pacifier, as it can spread germs if the pacifier falls on the ground, can cause a couple of sleepless nights when you want to take it away, and if you don't and let your baby use it for too long, it can cause problems with speech development and the forming of their mouth, which can result in crooked teeth. Talk to your partner and decide if you want to use one.

Swaddle

In the womb, babies don't have a lot of room for movement, which is why they often calm down when wrapped tightly in blankets.

Let them swing. Many parents swear by using a motorized swing. This calms the baby, as the movement is similar to what they felt in mom's womb when she was walking (or waddling closer to the end).

White noise

While in the womb, your baby constantly hears noises similar to white noise. This is why the sound of a vacuum cleaner, dishwasher, or washing machine can be so comforting for a baby. Doing the laundry can score you a double whammy of brownie points.

Put them in the car

This has proven to be highly effective when soothing a baby. Strap them into their car seat, leave mom at home to enjoy some quiet time, and go for a drive. If it's close to dinner time, go past a drive through restaurant and pick up something for supper—kudos for your incredible thinking right there!

BONDING WITH YOUR CHILD

After carrying the baby for nine months, giving birth to them, and then caring for them, your wife will already have a special bond with your little one. Since she'll likely be home on maternity leave, she'll also have more than enough time alone with the baby to cuddle and get to know their little quirks, likes, and dislikes.

This might not come as quickly for you, as you may only be home for a couple of days if you're lucky and won't have that automatic bonding that something like breastfeeding brings. You'll have to consciously work towards getting to know your tiny human. The best way to do this is to spend as much time with your baby as possible. Remember that quality is always more important than quantity, so even if you don't have much time to spend with your little one, make the most of what you have. The bond will come.

No matter how tired you might be after a long day at work and not sleeping properly since the baby's birth, you'll never have this time with your baby again. This sounds so cliché, I know, but it's the truth. Use every minute you can spare to bond with your little one. Before you know it, they will be teenagers with raging hormones, and you'll wish you had a sweet baby again.

As much as you want to sleep, getting up at night when your baby's fussy can be great for one-on-one bonding. They won't always want to drink when crying at night, often called the "witching hours." Sometimes, as we've mentioned, they will only want to be held and to feel secure. And, who better to make them feel safe than their superhero of a daddy? Soon, this little one will be your real-life sidekick, so set them up for this role now.

If your baby's wide awake at night and there doesn't seem to be much chance of getting them settled anytime soon, make the most of this time. Take the baby to the living room and put on your favorite tv show. At some point during their lives you'll have the opportunity, if you're into sports like me, to explain all the rules of your favorite game to your little one. And there's no rule against starting this super early in their lives.

When you speak to your baby, try your best to always look them in the eyes. A newborn's eyesight isn't fully developed, so bring your face close to theirs...As long as you are not sick, of course! Let your baby touch your face and pull your scruff. They are learning all there is to know about their daddy. Sing to your baby. They don't care whether you can hold a note or not. All they want is to hear your voice. When spending time with them, echo their little sounds and mirror their facial expressions. Your baby's trying to communicate, and this is their only means at such an early stage of life.

You might soon realize that you enjoy this bonding time so much that you may want to do this as often as possible. Invest in a baby sling where you can carry your little one as you go about your duties at home. This will keep your baby close and connected to you, free up your hands to get things done and give mom a much-needed break.

If your partner starts expressing milk for bottle feeding, or if you decide to feed the baby formula, get involved in these feeds from the get-go. Initially, your baby might cry or be fussy when you try to feed them, as they are used to mom giving them milk. You might also feel unsure of what to do. Whatever you do, don't give up and simply hand the baby back to mom. The more you do it, the easier it'll become for both you and your baby.

Always remember that no matter how much you try, there's no such thing as a perfect parent. All parents make mistakes. It's part of life, and you will also make mistakes. As long as your baby's happy and kept alive, you're doing a great job. Congratulate yourself for being the best dad you can be, and try every day to be better than the last.

BABYPROOF YOUR HOME

As your baby gets older and becomes more mobile, it's important to babyproof your home. One of the most important things to consider is making sure your electrical outlets are safe for your baby to be around. Various products on the market prevent your baby from sticking their little fingers in the outlets, jamming other things in there, or pulling a plug you're actively using. Go around your home and make notes of any electrical outlets in your baby's reach once they start crawling and walking. Make sure each one is covered.

You might think you don't need it, as you won't leave your baby unattended. However, trust me on this one. You have no idea how fast that little body can move. If you take your eyes off them for only a couple of seconds (while changing the channel on the television or checking a message on your phone), your baby might have moved to a danger zone, and you might just pull a muscle jumping up and running to keep them safe.

Also, look out for electrical wires that are hanging loose. Don't allow your baby to play tug of war with your television's cable. Chances are your baby will win the fight, with your television falling to pieces on the ground, possibly injuring your baby. You can get many cord rails or cable management boxes to reassure everything stays in place.

You can also look at different cabinets or magnetic locks to make sure your baby won't unpack your entire kitchen for you. These are particularly important for cupboards containing cleaning products or glassware. If you want to give your baby the chance to explore a little, you can leave your Tupperware cupboard unlocked. The baby won't harm themselves by unpacking this cupboard. Just look on the floor before entering the kitchen, as your baby might have turned your kitchen into a homemade obstacle course. You might harm yourself slipping on a plastic lid or board or trip over an empty cereal container stacked on top of another.

Once you're done with the electrical outlets and cables, look at anchoring your furniture. Many young children get seriously injured and can die from furniture falling onto them. For example, they don't understand the danger of pulling on a bookshelf and are more focused on discovering what is high on the bookshelf out of their reach. Children are natural climbers, and many can climb a bookshelf or chest of drawers before even walking properly. They will also use furniture to pull themselves up before standing up alone. You can use many brackets, wall mounts, and straps to anchor your furniture and appliances in position.

Regarding things you should put out of sight, don't leave any decorative items within your baby's reach, especially not glass or porcelain items that can break easily. Your friends and loved ones will know you used to have pretty things in your house, and they will understand why it has disappeared for now. Your baby's safety is much more important than having decorations in your home.

Another thing to consider is potted plants on the floors in your house. If your baby can reach them, they will likely dig out the soil in the pots, break off leaves, and even try to eat them. Remember that babies learn by putting things in their mouths. Many house plants are also poisonous if ingested, so removing this risk is always best by moving your potted plants out of reach.

Even loose throws and blankets can pose a risk. Your baby might get tangled in these, creating a risk of suffocation for young ones.

Your cushions will likely also get scattered all over your lounge floor, so unless you want to pick them up daily, it might be a good idea to store them for the next couple of months.

Toilet seat clips are handy to keep little fingers out. Remember what we said above about babies putting things in their mouths to learn? Nothing that goes in the toilet should ever go in your baby's mouth, so rather keep it locked. Also, don't leave your toilet brush beside the toilet for easy access. The bristles of those brushes might feel great for itchy gums. I don't think we need to expand on why this is a horrible idea.

If you have stairs or a fireplace in your house, baby gates can be great for keeping your baby safe. Their muscles are still developing, and they shouldn't be climbing stairs alone. Slipping and tumbling down a staircase can happen so quickly.

SEX AFTER BIRTH

Going through the first couple weeks of having a newborn, many men look forward to the six weeks mark. If your baby has gained healthy weight, your pediatrician might give you the good news that you can stop waking your baby up for night-time feeds. But that isn't all that happens at six weeks postpartum...

This is also when your wife will go for a postpartum checkup at her OB-GYN. Permitting no complications, the doctor might give your wife the all-clear for resuming intimacy.

If this is the case for your wife, it's excellent, as this means your wife's body has physically recovered from giving birth. However, don't ever pressure your wife to hop into bed. After everything she went through giving birth, she might not feel emotionally or mentally ready to allow anything close to her lady again just yet.

She might fear getting pregnant again. This fear isn't unfounded. Many women, even those breastfeeding, can resume ovulation before reaching the six-week mark. This means that if you don't use contraceptives, she can get pregnant again. This can be something neither of you might be ready for. Her OB-GYN will likely discuss contraceptives with her and will probably give your partner a script for the contraceptive of her choice. If she chooses to use this, help her get her medication from the pharmacy. While you're there, get a packet of condoms. Depending on the type of contraceptive she'll use, it might take a couple of weeks to fully take effect. The condoms might make her feel more comfortable if there's double protection.

Also, grab a bottle or two of water-based lubrication while at the pharmacy. Due to her hormones still adjusting after giving birth, and especially if she's breastfeeding, she might experience vaginal dryness, which can make sex very painful. Using lube can help with this, plus a lot of foreplay to increase natural arousal.

Even with doing all of this, she might not agree to have sex just yet. If you're upset or irritated by this, don't show it to your wife. She has put her body through hell carrying your baby. Have patience with her, and try other forms of intimacy. Hold her hand, tell her how much you appreciate her, cuddle with her, kiss her, and if she allows, touch her. Build up to penetrative intimacy again. Take things as slowly as she needs them to be.

Once you eventually get the okay to raise your sails, she might experience pain. Ensure you have good communication, or look at her face for any signs of pain or discomfort. Although most women only feel pain during the first couple of times of penetration, for some, it can be painful for up to three months postpartum. If the pain persists, take her to see her OB-GYN. There might be a cause that can easily be treated.

PRACTICAL NEW DAD TIP

Find your village by joining Facebook groups about parenting or becoming a dad. These groups are great ways of staying connected with other new dads who are also going through this crazy, beautiful process for the first time. Having someone who understands what you're going through is beyond helpful.

CONCLUSION

You now have all the knowledge you need to rock being a first-time dad. You've also learned valuable facts to make this journey easier and impress your wife. Having gained all this insight on how to help your partner during the pregnancy and delivery, and caring for your little baby, already puts you one step ahead of most other dads-to-be or new dads.

You're now aware of everything that can possibly go wrong during a pregnancy and when to rush your partner to the doctor. Conversely, you'll know what seemingly weird or odd things can be perfectly normal. You also understand what you can do to make this pregnancy easier for your wife and what you need to consider when budgeting for your baby's care.

Most importantly, you understand that it's normal to doubt your abilities as a father and that the fears you might be feeling are common. Taking care of your and your partner's mental health will be a top priority, not only during pregnancy but also after the birth of your tiny human. On top of that, you know what you should and definitely shouldn't do during the birth of your baby, as well as how to care for your little one afterward.

You might feel like you've gone through information overload. That's okay. There's a lot to learn; luckily, you can go over the appropriate chapters as you experience that part of your journey. Let's recap some of the important things we've discussed to make things a bit easier for you.

You might deal with a lot of fears, such as being too selfish to be a good dad, loving your job or hanging out with the guys more than your baby, losing your identity, experiencing FOMO while having a newborn in the house, and even getting a "dad bod." These fears are normal. However, remember that your body was also made for being a dad, and the lowering of your testosterone levels shortly before your baby's due is scientific proof.

You might go through times during this journey when you feel your mental health declining. You might be worried about the many changes this pregnancy will bring to your life. Knowing what to expect and planning for it can help reduce your anxiety. Talk to your wife and create your birth plan. Remember to make four copies of this plan.

Have patience with your wife while she's pregnant. Her body will go through hell, starting from around week six of pregnancy and lasting all the way to the birth of your little one. Her boobs will get extremely sore and swollen. She might suffer from morning (or all day) sickness. If she has weird cravings, just roll with it and buy her what she wants. Don't be sensitive to her mood swings. She can't help it. She may become forgetful. This strange phenomenon is called pregnancy brain. Help her through any difficulties in her pregnancy. Relieve her stress by giving a massage or making lists of what should be done.

If you want to impress your wife, plan a little getaway for the two of you before the baby's born. Go experience your babymoon! Find out what your wife would like to do, even if it's just relaxing in a hotel room with an air conditioner and room service.

Every pregnancy trimester comes with difficulties that your partner (and you) will go through. Important things that can happen during the first trimester include spotting, discharge, constipation, fatigue, frequent urination, and heartburn. Choose an OB-GYN to take care of your wife during the pregnancy and book an appointment. Get her a good prenatal vitamin. Get a healthy exercise routine going that you and your partner can do together. Consider how and when you want to share the news with the people you care about. And always be aware of any signs that indicate you need to rush to the doctor. These include heavy bleeding, severe abdominal pain, dizziness, and blurred vision.

The second trimester is often called the honeymoon phase of the pregnancy, as this is the time she'll feel best. She might even feel frisky during this stage. If this is the case, enjoy it. Your wife's tummy will grow fast, and people will start to notice the pregnancy. Your baby's kicks will become more robust, and soon your partner (and shortly after that, you) will feel these movements. There might be changes to her skin, including acne, stretch marks, dark marks on her face, and a dark line down her tummy. Now is a great time to look at taking birthing classes. During this trimester, you'll likely be able to find out the gender of your baby. Discuss with your wife if you want to know the gender and how you want to find out. Gender reveal parties are becoming very popular.

The third trimester will feel like a year, even though it's only three months long. Your wife will feel extremely uncomfortable. As this trimester progresses and the baby engages in the birth canal, she'll become even more uncomfortable. She'll experience pain at times due to her ligaments and muscles stretching. She might also start experiencing Braxton Hicks contractions. Read that again when it happens to your wife so you'll know whether your wife's experiencing these practice contractions or if it might be the start of true labor. Your wife will pee more than ever before. Stock up on twoply toilet paper. Do this now if you still need to get the baby's room ready. Spoil her with a pedicure, help her to shave, and practice your go-to answers to trick questions such as "Do I look fat?"

When your wife's in the third trimester, start thinking about baby names if you haven't already decided on one. Decide if you want to choose a godparent for your child or who you'll appoint as your baby's guardian. Make sure they are stipulated in your will.

As the pregnancy progresses, pack the bags for the hospital. Remember to pack everything your partner, your baby, and you will need during labor and for at least three days after the baby has been born. When the labor starts, know when to go to the hospital. Unless your OB-GYN advises otherwise, remember the 5-1-1 rule: If her contractions are five minutes apart, each contraction lasts for one minute and has continued for one hour. Apart from contractions, other signs of labor to look out for include her mucus plug coming out (pinkish-brown Jell-O-like blob), having the urgent need for continuous bowel movements, and her water breaking.

When you're in the delivery room, never make a face showing any disgust, never call anything gross, and never tell her how long she has been in labor. Instead, try to help her in any way you can. Place a cold, damp cloth on her face if she's sweating. Allow her to squeeze the life out of your hand, don't tell her that her pain isn't "that bad," and please don't tell her when to push. Leave that to the trained professionals.

If there are complications, your OB-GYN will recommend delivering the baby via a C-section, and this isn't something you should fear. Know, however, that your wife's physical recovery will be longer, so be ready to help her in any way you can.

Once your baby has been born, be the gatekeeper. Only allow visitors once your partner and baby have settled into the maternity ward and all three of you are up for it. Remember to always make sure all visitors wash their hands and that they have no contagious diseases. If in doubt, don't let them in.

If your wife decides to breastfeed the baby, help her by getting snacks and ensuring she drinks enough fluids. Get involved in the feeds by burping the baby after every feed. Be there for your partner emotionally. Breastfeeding can be difficult and exhausting.

Before you know it, you'll take your baby home. Continue with your gatekeeper duties, but accept help when you and your wife need it, especially if someone offers to bring you a meal. Help out with chores around the house. Spend time with your baby by doing skin-to-skin contact. Take charge of bath time. And remember the importance of self-care, both for you and for your wife. You've both been through a lot, and caring for a newborn isn't an easy task.

Remember that dads don't babysit their children. They parent them. Be involved from the start by changing diapers and knowing how to handle and calm your baby. Spend quality time with your baby to bond. As soon as your baby becomes mobile, baby proof the house. Being the protector of your family is now part of your duties as a dad. Make sure you do everything you should to make your home as safe as possible for your tiny treasure.

Now that you have all the tools, go out there and use them. Be the dad you've always wanted to be. You'll rock this!

If you enjoyed reading this book and found the information helpful in preparation for your journey, please leave a review on Amazon.

To my new friend, cheers to being a Dad! I know you will rock.

- Alex

PS - if you want to continue the "You Will Rock As a Dad!" Journey with me, you can purchase my 2nd book to this series now live on Amazon called, "You Will Rock As a Dad!: The Expert Guide to Your Baby's First Year and Everything New Fathers Need to Know"

Simply scan the QR link below to grab your copy:

REFERENCES

Anderson, J. (2021, June 9). *5 sweet ways for dad to bond with baby*. Today's Parent. https://www.todaysparent.com/family/parenting/dad-struggling-to-bond-withbaby/

Babychakra. (2020, June 11). *10 things you must do to support your pregnant wife*. Swirlster. https://swirlster.ndtv.com/wellness-mother/10-things-you-must-do-tosupport-your-pregnant-wife-2244348

Babylist. (2019, December 12). *Second trimester of pregnancy*. https://www.babylist.com/hello-baby/second-trimester

Barth, L. (2020, June 11). *Is pregnancy brain real?* Healthline. https://www.healthline.com/health/pregnancy/is-pregnancy-brain-real

Ben-Joseph, E. P. (2018). *Bringing your baby home*. Nemours Kids Health. https://kidshealth.org/en/parents/bringing-baby-home.html

Centers for Disease Control and Prevention. (2021, November 1). *Preterm birth*. https://www.cdc.gov/reproductivehealth/maternalinfanthealth/pretermbirth.htm

Coleman, P. A. (2020, May 5). *Building a birth plan: What expectant parents should include and consider*. Fatherly. https://www.fatherly.com/health-science/buildbirth-plan-pregnancy-expecting

DiDonato, T. E. (2014, January 10). *5 reasons why couples who sweat together, stay together*. Psychology Today. https://www.psychologytoday.com/blog/meet-catch-and-keep/201401/5-reasons-why-couples-who-sweat-together-stay-together

Dragon, N. (2016, October 11). *Why pregnancy can make you have weird cravings*. Intermountain Healthcare. https://intermountainhealthcare.org/blogs/topics/ intermountain-moms/2016/10/why-pregnancy-can-make-you-have-weird-cravings/

Dubner, S. J. (2011, June 23). *It takes a village*. Freakonomics. https://freakonomics.com/2011/06/it-takes-a-village/

Gomstyn, A. (2022). *More than baby blues: Recognizing and recovering from postpartum depression*. Aetna. https://www.aetna.com/health-guide/ understanding-and-overcoming-postpartum-depression.html

Government of Victoria. (2012). *Childbirth - Pain relief options*. Better Health

Channel. https://www.betterhealth.vic.gov.au/health/HealthyLiving/child birth- pain-reliefoptions

Health America. (n.d.). *Mental health and the new father.* https://mhanational. org/mental-health-and-new-father

Healthdirect Australia. (2022). *Mental well-being during pregnancy.* Pregnancy Birth and Baby. https://www.pregnancybirthbaby.org.au/mental-wellbe ing-duringpregnancy

Healthdirect Australia. (2020). *Third trimester.* Pregnancy Birth & Baby. https:// www.pregnancybirthbaby.org.au/third-trimester

Hirsch, L. (2022). *Cesarean sections (C-sections).* Nemours Kids Health. https:// kidshealth.org/en/parents/c-sections.html

Kreidman, J. (2019, November 15). *Tips for new dads in the delivery room* [Video]. YouTube. https://www.youtube.com/watch?v=8G4e_NUkIeQ

Krieger, L. (2022, April 9). *First week at home with your newborn baby.* BabyCenter. https://www.babycenter.com/baby/newborn-baby/newborn-baby_10345806

Marcin, A. (2020, January 2). *How soon can you find out the sex of your baby?* Healthline. https://www.healthline.com/health/pregnancy/when-can-you-find- outsex-of-baby

Mayo Clinic. (2018, September 1). *Postpartum depression.* https://www. mayoclinic.org/diseases-conditions/postpartum-depression/symptoms-causes/syc20376617

Mayo Clinic. (2021, April 14). *Premature birth.* https://www.mayoclinic.org/ diseasesconditions/premature-birth/symptoms-causes/syc-20376730

Mayo Clinic. (2022, March 9). *3rd-trimester pregnancy: What to expect.* https:// www.mayoclinic.org/healthy-lifestyle/pregnancy-week-by-week/ in-depth/pregnancy/art-20046767

McKay, B. (2013, December 12). *New dad survival guide: The mindset.* The Art of Manliness. https://www.artofmanliness.com/people/fatherhood/new-dad-survivalguide-the-mindset/

McKay, B. (2021, May 30). *New dad survival guide: The skillset.* The Art of Manliness. https://www.artofmanliness.com/people/fatherhood/new-dad-survival-guidethe-skillset/

Merrell, C. (2022, March 24). *23 tips for new fathers.* Owlet. https://www.owlet care. com/blog/23-tips-on-becoming-a-father-for-the-first-time

National Health Service. (2020, December 1). *Signs that labour has begun.* https://www.nhs.uk/pregnancy/labour-and-birth/signs-of-labour/signs-that labour-has-begun/

Procter & Gamble. (2021, November 22). *Hospital bag checklist—What to pack.*

Pampers. https://www.pampers.com/en-us/pregnancy/giving-birth/article /whatto-pack-in-your-hospital-bag-go-bag-checklist

Rogers-Anderson, S. (n.d.). *10 expert tips to choosing a baby name*. The Tot. https://www.thetot.com/mama/10-expert-tips-for-choosing-a-baby-name/

Sandbox & Co. (n.d.). *Meaning and origin of Cameron*. Family Education. https://www.familyeducation.com/baby-names/name-meaning/ cameronMental

Schools, D. (2018, September 24). *My 6 brutally honest fears about becoming a first-time dad*. Medium. https://daveschools.medium.com/my-6-brutally-honest-fearsabout-becoming-a-first-time-dad-9464dcadc3af

Stewart, R. (2016, June 14). *Soon-to-be dads: How to help – And what not to say – During pregnancy*. UT Southwestern Medical Center. https://utswmed.org/ medblog/ fathers-guide-to-pregnancy/

Taylor, S. (2017, June 21). *The tricky task of choosing the right godparents for your baby*. Babyology. https://babyology.com.au/parenting/relationships/how-to- choosegodparents-for-your-baby/

Tiu, A. (2021a, April 11). *How to baby-proof your home 2021* [Video]. YouTube. https://www.youtube.com/watch?v=48BH4EuWTl4

Tiu, A. (2021b, May 25). Sex after birth – Postpartum intimacy for new moms/dads [Video]. YouTube. https://www.youtube.com/watch?v=JDIOz9jUGE4

Turner, A. (2020, June 23). Delivery room tips for dads: 5 things not to do in labor [Video]. YouTube. https://www.youtube.com/watch?v=VtjfS96qdnE

Watson, S. (2020a, July 16). *First trimester of pregnancy: What to expect*. WebMD. https://www.webmd.com/baby/guide/first-trimester-of-pregnancy

Watson, S. (2020b, August 25). *Second trimester of pregnancy*. WebMD. https:// www.webmd.com/baby/guide/second-trimester-of-pregnancy

WebMD. (n.d.). *C-section: What can I expect?* https://www.webmd.com/baby/ whathappens-during-c-section#1

Welch, N. (2010, March 26). *A dad's point of view*. New Parent. https://newpar ent.com/mom/a-dads-point-of-view1/

BOOK 2: YOU WILL ROCK AS A DAD!

THE EXPERT GUIDE TO YOUR BABY'S FIRST YEAR AND EVERYTHING NEW FATHERS NEED TO KNOW

Alex Grace

INTRODUCTION

Remember the day you stared down at those two pink lines on the pregnancy test, your heart racing with a mix of excitement and terror? Fast forward to what seemed like both the longest and shortest nine months of your life, and you're now in your baby's first year! How time flies! Every first-time dad has felt that rush of emotions, wondering if he's up to the task or feeling like he has absolutely no idea what he's doing. The truth is, you likely don't have a clue about what you need to do or how you should do it. And how could you? For the first time, you're suddenly responsible for a brand-new life and may even wonder how such big hands will be able to handle such a tiny body.

For many men, including myself, fatherhood starts out feeling like an emotional rollercoaster that you both enjoy and fear. In an attempt to become the perfect dad, you might rush online to research everything you need to know. Unfortunately, due to the vast amount of information and opinions just a click away, you're most likely left feeling more unsure of what to do than ever before. Many of your family members or friends may also offer their well-meaning but unsolicited advice, which might completely go against what you read online. This may leave you feeling like you're drowning in confusion, completely overwhelmed.

You may deeply fear the loss of your identity and time. The transition from having ample personal time to dedicate most of it to a newborn is drastic. Gone are the days when you could simply stop at the local bar for a beer with your friends, get in a good long session at the gym, or just spend some alone time whenever you want, without having to rush home to fulfill your share of the parenting duties.

This feeling of being trapped in your new role in which you likely doubt your own capabilities and adequacy can easily lead to "new dad anxiety." You may deeply fear making mistakes, not being supportive enough for your partner, or not bonding properly with your baby. You may even question whether you can do it at all as you must suddenly become an expert in changing diapers, handling throw-ups, or soothing a crying baby at 3 am.

While all these changes in your life are taking place, you may also fear the future of your relationship with your partner. Before becoming parents, you could simply enjoy spending time in each other's company without sharing the other with anyone. With the arrival of a new baby, the dynamics in your relationship with your partner can change drastically. You may worry that your sex life may be over forever, as both you and your partner may be too tired or overwhelmed to even think about getting it on, especially during the stressful early months of parenthood.

Luckily, these overwhelming fears over your new role and responsibilities don't have to take away from the joy fatherhood can bring. You can become the type of father you've always believed you could and will be. By becoming more intentional with the role you play, your involvement, and the impact you have on your child's life, you will empower not just yourself but also your child to thrive.

In the second series of *You Will Rock As a Dad!* we will be discussing everything you need to know from practical advice on baby care to the emotional and psychological challenges new dads face. This will help to ensure you feel supported, informed, and ready to embrace fatherhood, as it will answer all those burning questions about the first year and offer real solutions to those everyday baby challenges.

ABOUT ME

I am very excited to be helping you along your new journey. If you've read my first book, I want to say welcome back! If you are new to the "You Will Rock As a Dad! Series" I want to say "nice to meet you, new dad!" A little bit about me, I've grown up in a sports family where teamwork and collaboration ruled the house. I enjoyed the role of "fun uncle" for many years before I became a father. I thought I would easily ace the new role, as over the years, I was the go-to family member for my nieces and nephews, and had extensive background within the childcare system. I thought to myself, "if I love being around children, surely having my own would be a piece of cake."

Unfortunately, I didn't anticipate the absolute shock to the system that becoming a dad could bring. It's not like working in childcare where you could have fun teaching and guiding children but then send them home to their parents at the end of the day while you enjoy the freedom of blowing off steam. Suddenly, you need to become the responsible one who has to put your child and family above anything else.

After I eventually overcame this shock and learned to manage my high levels of "new dad anxiety," I decided to focus on doing the little things right. That helped to take the stress out of the tasks and before I knew it, I settled into my new role and already started nagging my wife to try for another baby, full of dreams of creating my own little sports team at home.

Now, I want to help you. I am passionate about sharing my knowledge and experience with other dads to make this journey not only easier but also more enjoyable for them. You may have already started this journey with me in my debut best-selling book, *You Will Rock As a Dad! The Expert Guide to First-Time Pregnancy and Everything New Fathers Need to Know.* In this book, we discussed everything you need to know about being the perfect partner to your pregnant counterpart (and score massive brownie points in the process). Now, we'll focus on the first year of your baby's life and how you can go from being an average Joe to a true super dad for your little one. So, grab your cape, and let's get started. Because one thing is for certain, now that we are on this journey together, I know you will rock as a dad. Better yet, when you're done reading this book, you're going to have what I like to call, "rockin' dad energy". The dad jokes are starting!

Let's dive in.

CHAPTER ONE

EMBRACING THE CHAOS OF LIFE WITH A NEWBORN

Remember those calm Sunday mornings, coffee in hand, peacefully browsing through the news, or bingeing your favorite series? Your baby, with their round-the-clock demands, has different plans for you! Welcome to the first month of fatherhood, where 'unexpected' is the new norm. But here's a secret: It's the most fulfilling chaos you'll ever embrace.

If you are prepared for the challenges that you may face during this whirlwind of a month, you'll empower yourself to handle anything, regardless of how unexpected it may seem. This will help you to make sure your brand-new family thrives.

FROM EXPECTATIONS TO REALITY

Being a dad involves far more than simply sowing your seed and letting your partner squeeze the life out of your hand during childbirth. It also involves much more than just working to financially provide for your family. In today's world, the traditional notion of men being the sole bread-winners while women solely manage childcare and house-hold tasks is a thing of the past.

These days, it's common for both parents to work full-time, which means all household chores and parenting duties ideally are split between both parents. You both won't just have to provide for your family financially but also play an active role in the daily running of your home and raising your child. The demands placed on dads in modern life are becoming more than ever before, which can easily result in feelings of guilt over either not bringing in enough money for their partners to stay at home, if their partner chooses to, or not contributing enough to the household on an emotional level.

Research done by Lancaster University found that men also don't get the credit they deserve for their role in caring for their children (Brindle, 1999). Families mostly focus on the bigger tasks, such as cooking, caring for young babies, and helping older children with homework. In many homes, these are tasks that are fulfilled by the mothers, while many dads are regarded as the "fun parent" who play games with their children, help them with sports, or drive them to and from activities. Even though they play an important role in their children's lives, the input of mothers is often regarded as more important.

Unfortunately, the business world has yet to catch on to the change in parenting roles of modern-day dads, compared to the previous generation. Many companies still discriminate against men who want to take parental leave when their children are sick or have an event to attend at school.

Social media can make things even worse, particularly when you start to compare your parenting style and influence as a dad to what you see on social media. People seldom post the truth about their lives. Instead, what makes it onto social media pages are often heavily edited videos or photos. You may admire the dad in the laughing videos while he plays sports with his son in the park or quick selfies of stroller rides. But, what you don't see are the tantrums that happen when the son accidentally steps in dog feces during the mini-football match or how the dad had to carry his son down the street as he suddenly got too tired to move but had the energy to kick and scream while being carried off. So, when you compare yourself and your role as a dad to what you see on social media, you'll often compare yourself to an idealist view of fatherhood, which is far removed from reality.

When you're involved in your children's upbringing and share the parenting duties, you'll not only have a happier partner but your children will also reap the benefits. Studies have found that children whose fathers are actively involved in their lives generally do better at school, are healthier, are more disciplined, and have a reduced risk of getting themselves in trouble with the law (FamilyEducation Editorial Staff, 2022).

THE POWER OF PATIENCE: ACCEPTING THE UNEXPECTED

I'm sure you've seen this scene play out a few times: A father is standing in line at a store with his toddler throwing a full-on tantrum, wanting a new toy or candy. At first, you can see the father is trying his best to stay calm and not give in to the tantrum. However, after a while, his patience runs out and he either loses it by scolding his child and dragging them out of the shop, or giving in to the tantrum and buying his child the toy or candy they wanted to begin with.

Before your child gets to this level of unrelenting and strong-willed public performances, you might have planned how you're going to deal with them and stay calm at all times. I was one of them. I always believed I knew how I would handle my children when they would throw tantrums. Unfortunately, I had no idea what I was in for and I soon realized that my plans were often just as ridiculous as the reasons for their behavior. Just like the gas in my car, I ran out of patience too many times, because I never prepared myself to accept the unexpected. And, just like it's necessary to have that gas in your car if you want to drive somewhere, patience is a necessity in parenthood. Unfortunately, this is something many parents lack.

So, before we go any further, let's first look at patience. The Merriam-Webster dictionary defines being patient as "going through your struggles calmly and without complaining about what's happening, or remaining steadfast despite the struggles you may endure" (*Patient*, n.d.). When you're a parent, especially when you're just starting on this journey, you may struggle to cope with some of your challenges, which can include difficulty consoling your crying baby, burning dinner because you're busy tending to your child, dividing your chores and duties with your partner, or even just the lack of freedom that typically comes with having a newborn in the house. When you respond to these challenges by showing your irritation, complaining, or yelling, you'll only end up increasing your stress levels, which will make the situation significantly more difficult (speaking from experience here).

While there are many ways in which you can work on becoming more patient, I found a combination of accepting there will always be unexpected events and seeing the bigger picture in everything you do. Once I was able to change my mindset from trying to fight the unexpected events to simply accepting that there would always be things out of my control and that I needed to go more with the flow, I was able to become more emotionally stable, even in these difficult times. In my view, patience is a combination of both your attitude in how you choose to see things and your ability to choose how you want to respond. Simply put, patience is broken down to attitude and response. Until the big corporations figure out how to bottle and sell patience (I know many parents who are desperately hoping for that to happen), becoming more patient will require continuous effort.

Think of your approach to fatherhood as a toolbox; your attitude is the key tool that can either build a solid foundation or create obstacles, similar to self-fulfilling prophecies. If you go into parenting believing you won't have the patience to deal with the many instances that will test your patience, then I can almost guarantee you that your patience will fail you more often than not. No matter how much we might want to have it all, parenting comes with many sacrifices that may seem hard to make now but will be well worth it in the end. So, if you start this journey with an open mindset and accept the unexpected, you will be able to deal with your challenges a lot more effectively.

When you choose to see the bigger picture, you'll realize that this challenging moment that's currently testing your patience is nothing but a small irritation in your bigger journey. You don't have to turn it into a massive road bump that will damage your relationship with your partner or your children. Instead, if you can embrace the power of patience, you'll build the foundation for lifelong happiness with your partner and children.

For the first week or so after bringing our first baby home, I was bursting with pride. I was incredibly proud of my wife for sacrificing her body to bring a new life into the world. I was proud of my role in creating this life. And, I was so in love with our baby that I would spend hours looking at him, counting his 10 toes and fingers repeatedly. I was also very impressed with how well he slept at night, (at first), thinking we were going to ace parenthood.

Alas, our home's brief stint of solitude had an expiration date shorter than a microwave popcorn timer. Soon, our sweet little baby discovered his lungs and voice, and my wife and I would spend many sleepless nights passing him to and fro between us, desperately hoping that the other one would have the magic touch to get him quiet. I'm not going to lie to you, this tested our patience and there were many times my wife and I wanted to both sit in a corner and join our baby in crying. In Chapter 4, we'll discuss tips on how to calm yourself and your baby during these difficult times.

While you need to stay patient with your children, you'll also need an extra bucket of patience with your partner. She has been to hell and back to bring a new life into this world, not just physically but emotionally and mentally as well. Now that there's a new life to care for, it's possible she may doubt herself and her ability to be a good mother. Don't we all a little when we're new at something? You need to be patient with her when she struggles to cope with her new duties and just doesn't get to the chores on her to-do list. Cut her some slack. Just like it's not easy being a first-time dad, becoming a first-time mother can be a terrifying but highly rewarding experience.

SKIN-TO-SKIN, BATHING, AND SUPPORTING THEIR NECK

During the first month of life, most of a newborn's movements are a result of reflexes, particularly in their arms, legs, and face. Yes, Dad, those sweet smiles that you may be so excited to see aren't actually smiles just yet, but keep looking and photographing. Their deliberate movements will mostly be around sucking and swallowing. They may also turn their heads slightly in search of milk and if you put something in their hands, they may grasp it. As your baby grows and their movements become more coordinated, keep a watchful eye on what they grab as there will come a time when they'll put everything they touch in their mouths, even a dirty old rag.

They won't be able to see anything further than a few inches from their faces, so hold your baby as often as you can, particularly when they're awake, to help them connect your face with your voice that they'll know so well by now. By the end of the first month, they should be able to focus on still and sometimes moving objects. If you've been placing your baby on their tummy regularly for tummy time, they may be able to lift their heads off the ground by the end of the first month. We'll also discuss tummy time in more detail in Chapter 4.

During the first few months, your baby will spend most of their time sleeping. In fact, most newborns sleep for up to 16 hours a day. Unfortunately, this won't be a straight sleep cycle. Most newborns won't sleep longer than 30 minutes to an hour at a time. They may also confuse their day and night sleep cycles. We'll discuss tips on how to improve your baby's sleep cycle later in this chapter.

You should never be afraid of picking your baby up. Yes, their bodies may seem small and fragile but they are a lot stronger and tougher than they may seem. The most important thing to keep in mind is to always support their necks when you pick them up. At this stage, the muscles in their neck will be too weak to support the weight of their head. You can do this by always keeping one hand under their necks when you pick them up, and supporting their bodies by placing your other hand under their butt.

Never shake your baby, whether during play or in frustration. This can result in shaken baby syndrome, which basically means bruising or damage to the brain bouncing back and forth in the skull. In severe cases, shaken baby syndrome can cause brain damage or even be fatal. When you place your baby in their stroller, car seat, or any other chairs you might have for them, you should always strap them in securely to keep them safe and prevent the likelihood of this syndrome.

Building a strong bond can begin right from the moment your baby arrives by gently cradling them, caressing their tiny bodies, or providing a soothing massage. Skin-to-skin contact can also hold many benefits, such as calming your baby, regulating their body temperature, and even boosting their immune system. To do this, take off your shirt and let your baby, dressed in only their diaper, lie tummy-down on your chest. If you want to flex some muscles to impress your partner with your new "dad bod," go for it (sarcasm intended here!).

During the first few days, your baby only needs sponge baths. This is to ensure their umbilical cord stump stays as dry as possible so that it can fall off. If your baby was circumcised, you'll also want to keep their penis as dry as you can until it heals. Once you can bath the baby, get everything ready before you take them to the bathroom (or baby bath, if you wish to wash them in the room.) Always add cold water to the bath first before you top it up with hot water until you get the desired temperature. This is to avoid burns in case your baby accidentally comes in contact with the water. Make sure you have their body wash, face cloth, cotton balls, towel, clothes, diaper, and diaper clean ready.

When you place your baby in the bath, support their neck with your hand and use your middle finger and thumb to keep their ears closed and reduce water entering their ear canal. Use new cotton balls to clean the skin around their eyes, a fresh one for each eye. After that, you can clean their bodies while always supporting their necks.

Remember, every baby is unique and may not follow these general guidelines or tips exactly. If you have any concerns about your baby's development or behavior, it's always a good idea to consult with a healthcare professional.

FEEDING 101: BREASTFEEDING VERSUS FORMULA

During the first six months, milk will be your baby's primary food source. After that, you'll gradually start to introduce soft foods while still giving them milk to supplement their feeds. This might sound simple enough but the milk you choose to feed your baby can be one of the first major decisions you'll make as a parent.

There are two options of milk for a newborn: breast milk and formula. While breastmilk will always be the perfect food for your baby, not all new mothers are able to breastfeed their babies. Some may have serious challenges, such as having inverted nipples or other medical conditions that may make breastfeeding impossible, while others may simply not get the hang of it or have enough milk for their babies.

My wife was really adamant about breastfeeding our children but she had many challenges. She first struggled to get the baby to latch and ended up with sore, cracked nipples. She went through many tubes of nipple cream to try to treat her nipples but she ended up bleeding through those cracks. Then, her milk never came in properly. As a result, our baby was underfed and his blood sugar dropped to dangerously low levels. The doctors gave her medication to try to increase her milk supply and recommended that she express milk—pumping milk out using either a hand pump, electrical pump, or even squeezing by hand—every hour while supplementing the feeds with formula. For the first three weeks of our firstborn's life, my wife spent most of the time in the room expressing milk, only to gain two ounces of milk per day, which was barely enough for a single feed. To make matters worse, she developed a cold, which she passed on to our baby. His pediatrician then explained she had two options: Either continue in this way and risk our baby, who didn't have a strong immune system yet, getting sicker, or stop breastfeeding completely and treat her own illness. She was absolutely devastated and felt like she was failing our baby. Luckily, our baby thrived on formula.

After she gave birth to our second baby, she wanted to give breastfeeding a go a second time but struggled again with latching and not having enough milk. With the second baby, we made sure we had formula in the house as a backup in case we needed it. So, as we walked into the house after returning from the hospital, I walked straight to the kitchen to clean and sterilize the baby bottles. My wife made peace with the fact that she wouldn't ever breastfeed her children successfully. I was incredibly proud of how she handled this challenging situation.

Never force your partner into a specific way of feeding or make her feel bad if she struggles with breastfeeding. In a few years' time, your baby will put mud and dead insects in their mouths regardless of the type of milk you gave them as an infant. I remember one night as we sat down for dinner, our youngest child literally scooped up a dead fly with her mouth. I lost my appetite completely that meal. But, it just showed again that you should never put too much pressure on yourself or your partner on how you "should" feed your baby. As long as your baby is fed, you're doing a great job as a parent, not that I recommend feeding your baby dead flies, obviously.

Let's look at the pros and cons of each type of feeding, starting with breastfeeding. This will not only help your partner in making the decision on how to feed your baby but you'll also score serious brownie points with your knowledge of the different methods of feeding your baby.

All You Need to Know About Breastfeeding

Nursing a baby can be an incredible way for your partner to bond with your little one. Breastmilk contains all the nutrients and antibodies your baby will need, which can boost your baby's immune system and help their body fight off infections a lot easier. It's made up of different components, such as lactose, fat, and protein (whey and casein), which makes it easy for a baby's immature digestive system to digest the milk. This then results in fewer cases of diarrhea and constipation in breastfed babies.

Another benefit of breastfeeding is its practicality. Your baby's milk will always be ready for them at the perfect temperature, so no matter where you may go or how long you may be out of the house, as long as your partner is there, your baby can be fed. This can also make nighttime feeds a lot easier, as there will be no need to wash and sterilize bottles and bottle teats or warm up a bottle in the middle of the night.

Your financial situation can also impact your decision on how to feed your baby. Breastmilk is obviously free, whereas formula can do a serious number on your budget, especially if you didn't plan on buying formula to begin with. What's more, since breastfed babies' immune systems develop quicker, they will be less likely to get sick, which means fewer trips to the doctor, copayments for these specialists, or money spent on medication. Since babies have many needs that can easily cost hundreds of dollars a month, the cost of formula and other potential expenses are things that should definitely be considered when you decide how you want to feed your baby. Trust me, every cent saved can help a great deal when unexpected emergencies happen, such as if your baby needs fancy ointment for a skin condition or a nappy rash.

In general, breastfed babies adjust to eating solids a lot easier. This is because the taste of their milk will vary according to their mother's diet. Since they are exposed to different flavors a lot earlier in life, they tend to accept the different flavors of solids more easily as well.

Breastfeeding can have amazing benefits for your partner as well. If she's physically able to do this, it can give her confidence as a new mother an amazing boost. Breastfeeding can also help to shrink her uterus back to its pre-pregnancy size a lot quicker. Some studies suggest breastfeeding can lower the risk of high blood pressure, breast cancer, ovarian and uterine cancer, cardiovascular disease, and diabetes (Ben-Joseph, 2018).

Unfortunately, as was the case with my wife, many women struggle to nurse their babies or might not be able to do so at all. Some medical conditions, such as anything that requires chemotherapy, HIV/Aids, taking certain medications, or even some infections, can make breastfeeding unsafe for the baby. Also, women who have had any form of surgery on their breasts, which includes breast reductions and enlarge-ments, may struggle more with breastfeeding.

Your partner's lifestyle should be considered when you make this decision. While it's a fact that breastfeeding can be very convenient as the milk is always ready for your baby to drink, breastfed babies typically drink a lot more often than formula-fed babies as they digest breastmilk a lot faster than formula: On average, newborns that are breastfed drink every two hours, while formula-fed babies can go for three to four hours between feeds. If your wife has to return to work shortly after having a baby and can't express milk or feed your baby every two hours, this type of feeding might not work for her.

New mothers who breastfeed should also take more care of what they eat or drink as everything they consume can be passed onto the baby. For example, fish can be a no-go due to the level of mercury it may contain, tomato and chocolate can make her milk more acidic, caffeine can cause restless-ness in your baby, and alcohol—yes, even after giving it up for nine months, should still be off-limits for breastfed babies—can result in fetal alcohol syndrome, which can have serious and lifelong implications for your baby.

Formula: A Healthy Alternative

Formula is infant milk that's commercially prepared and contains most of the nutrients and vitamins contained in breast milk. Again, just like you need to set the right expecta-tions for fatherhood, the formula that's available these days has evolved tremendously. If your partner can't breastfeed, your baby will do just fine with a good formula that contains all the proteins, fats, and sugars they need.

Formula feeding will require more preparations in that bottles need to be washed, sterilized, and warmed for your baby to enjoy. However, it does give a lot more flexibility. Feeding a baby when you're in public can be easier than breastfeeding as your partner won't have to search for a quiet space or worry about covering herself up as the baby drinks. Other people can also help with the feeds, which means you, as the father, can join in on the precious bonding time during a feed. If your wife has to return to work, sending formula with her to the daycare or to the day mother who will look after them is easier than having to worry about making sure you have enough expressed milk available for the day.

If you do go for formula, it's best to create a routine early on of washing and sterilizing bottles. You may want to get a few bottles so you don't have to wash immediately after a feed to have the bottle ready for the next one. Always making sure you have bottles ready can take some planning and organization but once you get into the rhythm of how you want to do it, you'll find it will become easier and easier.

Since formula takes longer to digest than breastmilk, they not only need to drink less often, as we've mentioned, but they also tend to sleep better and may even start to sleep through the night within the first few months. Your partner's diet won't impact your baby's nutrition if they are formula-fed. Therefore, communication with your partner is key to planning what course of action is best for your child's feeds.

Unfortunately, no matter how much work is put into developing formula, none of the antibodies that are found in breast milk can be manufactured for formula. This type of milk, therefore, doesn't boost the baby's immune system like breastmilk does. It can also take time to find the right formula for your baby. There are many different formulas available and it can take a few tries before you find one that works for your baby. The wrong formula can cause constipation, gassiness, and even diarrhea. Your child's pediatrician or lactation consultant will be able to recommend a formula they believe will work best for your baby but even with their expert advice, it can be a lengthy and costly period of trial and error.

Always keep an open mind when it comes to feeding your baby. As was the case with us and my wife who really wanted to breastfeed, your initial decision may not be realistic. Accept the unexpected and if you need to change your feeding plans, do it without any feelings of guilt for you or your partner. Choosing between breast milk and formula is like deciding between a homemade chef's special straight from mom or a gourmet takeout option—both have their unique flavors but it's all about what suits you and your baby.

TEST YOUR NEW DAD IQ

Now that we've discussed everything you need to know to be a stand-out dad to your newborn, let's check what you can remember. If you struggle with any of these questions, refer back to the various sections in the chapter to refresh your memory.

1. How often should your newborn feed?
2. Why should you adjust your expectations?
3. Why is it important to accept the unexpected?
4. Is it okay to sit back and relax while your partner takes care of the baby and all the household chores?
5. Can you give your partner a glass of wine while she's breastfeeding the baby?

Now that you're diving deep into the unpredictable waters of the first month, you might be sensing some unfamiliar emotions creeping in. Some mix of excitement, fear, and overwhelming responsibility? All normal. Welcome to the world of "New Dad Anxiety." But don't fret my new friend; in our next chapter, we're diving deep into it, helping you navigate and emerge stronger.

CHAPTER TWO

THE MYSTERY OF "NEW DAD ANXIETY"

I'll never forget the day my wife and I announced our first pregnancy to our friends. While most of them immediately congratulated us, there was one friend who became white and even looked a bit nauseous. By that time, he was already a father of three, all under the age of four. I could actually feel him shaking when he shook my hand, and with a nervous smile, he told me, "Good luck. It's a rollercoaster."

At that stage, I thought he referred only to the exciting changes that having our first baby would bring to our lives. It was only after our baby was born that I understood the many dips this rollercoaster takes, which can easily result in mental health struggles, or as I like to call it, "New Dad Anxiety."

If you've already had a taste of this type of anxiety, please understand you're not alone. Did you know that up to 10% of new dads experience paternal postpartum depression, and many more encounter heightened anxiety? (Horsager-Boehrer, 2021). This isn't just about a few sleepless nights; it's a deeper concern that's often overlooked. There are many reasons why you may feel particularly anxious or even depressed during this time, such as extreme fears over your new role and whether you have what it takes to be a good dad. And, let me tell you, by the end of this book I know you will.

Unfortunately, if you don't find a way to navigate your mental health and manage your anxiety and depressive thoughts more effectively, you may rob yourself of the greatest gift anyone can ever get: Bonding with your new family. So, let's unravel the mystery behind "New Dad Anxiety" and understand you're not alone in this journey.

WHAT IS "NEW DAD ANXIETY?"

You may have heard about baby blues and postpartum depression, where new mothers are experiencing extremely low and sometimes even depressive moods. This typically starts within the first few weeks after giving birth and can last for up to 1 year. If your partner struggles with this, you should do your best to be extra supportive and attentive toward their needs. Or perhaps you might be the one who needs an extra hug at the end of a tough day. And, let me tell you, fellas, there's nothing wrong with admitting that.

Postpartum depression can also occur in dads, particularly by the time your child is three to six months old (Horsager-Boehrer, 2021). I prefer calling it "New Dad Anxiety," as that is how I experienced it. Working in child care and being a coach in multiple different sports (soon, my kids will pick up golf and pickle ball), I couldn't remember a time when I didn't look forward to one day becoming a dad. When my wife revealed those double-positive lines on the pregnancy test, I was happier than a cat in an endless yarn pit, and I've never seen a cat happier than me since my first teenage kiss! But, a few weeks after the birth of our son, I felt myself lying to my family and friends every time I responded with the standard "good" or "great" when they asked me how things were going.

The reality was that while my wife and I were getting by, things were challenging. I was struggling to manage my work, the endless supply of diapers to be changed and bottles to be washed, and then the more mundane stuff, like helping to cook meals and picking up the dog poop outside. There were days when I felt like just throwing away the dirty dishes instead of just washing them. I know I sound dramatic, but it's true. I was dog-tired (and you might be too, but it's okay). I felt like I was in over my head and going to work in the mornings started to feel like a day-long vacay.

I can't even tell you how many nights I lay awake (even though I desperately needed sleep in between feeds) worrying about how I was going to cope with everything I had on my plate, my relationship with my wife, balancing being a new father, trying to be a person, and raising an entire human being. The combination of my severe sleep deprivation and stress caused me to become extremely irritable. I got so bad that not even kicking a few soccer balls on an open field (this was always my way of relaxing) could help me become a likable person again.

One night our son was extra cranky. Perhaps he could sense my high levels of tension. My wife was exhausted, so I offered to take him. It wasn't like I was going to sleep any way. I tried everything to get our son to settle: I rocked him for hours, sang for him (in retrospect, my singing could've made him more upset), and gave him tummy rubs, but nothing worked. Around 4 in the morning, I lost it. I grabbed his bouncy seat, dragged it to the living room, and put a movie on the TV, loud enough to drown out his moans. Eventually, we both fell asleep.

When I woke up on the couch and saw my baby sleeping like a little angel in his bouncy chair, I felt like I'd officially earned the "worst dad in the world" trophy. I knew something had to change, but I had no idea of how to pull myself together. I pulled my phone out to research and was amazed to discover that many other new dads had similar experiences.

I remember reading some of the online posts I found out loud to my wife, telling her that I couldn't believe that paternal postpartum depression was actually a real thing. She didn't quite look as shocked as I expected her to be. Instead, she just told me that it's because there are too many men like me who shy away from properly acknowledging our feelings and fears. This is one of the reasons why I prefer to call it "New Dad Anxiety" rather than postpartum depression.

That day, I promised myself that I would change. I wanted to be better. I wanted to teach my son that it's okay to be scared or emotional at times. I wanted to be the role model he deserved. Gaining this understanding was life-changing for me, as it may also be for you. It might even have saved my marriage.

SIGNS OF "NEW DAD'S ANXIETY"

While there are many similarities between maternal post-partum depression and "New Dad Anxiety," such as fatigue and appetite changes, crying is one of the most common symptoms new moms experience. This is often not present in men, most likely because to a large degree, society has encouraged us not to cry, show emotion, or talk about our feelings. We are a strange species, aren't we?

As a result of this stone-age way many of us have been raised, our symptoms of "New Dad Anxiety" can often show up completely different, which can make it more damaging to those around us than if we could just muster the courage to openly talk about what we feel. Some of the most common symptoms of "New Dad Anxiety" include:

- Anger outbursts or violent behavior.
- Impulsive or risky behavior, which can include overconsumption of alcohol or usage of drugs.
- Severe irritability.
- Excessive worry.
- Panic attacks.
- Lack of motivation and poor concentration.
- Withdrawal from relationships.
- Not enjoying the things you used to like.

- Physical symptoms, such as digestion issues, headaches, stomach pain, and muscle cramps.
- Sexual dysfunction.
- Sense of impending doom.
- Suicidal thoughts.

If your partner experiences baby blues or maternal postpartum depression, you should keep an extra close eye on your mood. Studies found that the partners of new mothers struggling with these mood disorders are twice as likely to develop "New Dad Anxiety" than the new dads whose partners' mental health is good during this time (Villano, 2018).

CAUSE AND TRIGGERS: WHY DO WE FEEL THIS WAY?

Apart from being more likely to experience "New Dad Anxiety" if your partner's mental health is also struggling, there are many other factors that could contribute to your anxiety getting the better of you, such as:

- **Hormones:** As your partner gets closer to giving birth, you will experience hormonal changes, particularly a drop in testosterone. This is your body preparing to nurture and care for your newborn. Unfortunately, the downside to lower testosterone levels can be feelings of depression, which can add to your "New Dad Anxiety."
- **Feeling disconnected:** Your partner starts to bond with the baby while she is still pregnant and if she is on maternity leave after giving birth, she will spend

a lot more time with your baby. This can result in you feeling excluded and disconnected from both your baby and your partner.

- History of mental health conditions: If you have a history of anxiety disorder or depression, your risk of developing "New Dad Anxiety" will be greatly increased.

- **Sleep deprivation:** It's no secret that parents of a newborn won't get the amount of sleep they may need to cope with the challenges that come with being a new parent. When we are tired, we tend to be more cranky, which won't help the state of our mental health at all.

- **Financial struggles:** Babies can do a number on your budget, especially if there are unexpected expenses you didn't plan for. If your money is already tight before having your little one, these additional expenses can cause a lot of stress.

- **Changes in your relationship:** There's no way to escape certain changes in your relationship with your partner. Together, you'll be responsible for a brand-new life, which naturally means less time together. Your baby's cries may also interrupt any alone time you might have planned to spend together, which can be very frustrating for both of you. While these changes can put even the strongest relationships to the test, they may also create an even deeper bond and love between you and your partner.

- **Lack of freedom:** Your life will change drastically after your baby has been born. If you're used to doing your own thing whenever you want, it can be incredibly frustrating when you need to rush home after work to take care of your baby and do chores. Your time won't be your own anymore; it's best to accept this sooner rather than later.

- **Not getting enough support:** If you aren't lucky enough to have a strong support system you can rely on during this time to give advice or look after the baby while you and your partner enjoy a much-needed break, your frustration levels may be even higher than normal. All the pressure will then be on you and your partner to not only take care of your baby but also support each other.

- **Not having time off:** Many new dads are hesitant to ask for time off from work after the birth of a baby as they may fear that it may either make them seem weak or even it may affect their chances of getting a promotion. However, spending more time at home after the birth of your little one can do wonders to reduce your "New Dad Anxiety."

As if this list of potential causes isn't long enough already, you can add the many fears most new parents experience during the first few months of parenthood to it as well. Some of these emotional rollercoaster fears can include:

- **The unknown:** Until you're actually a dad, you won't ever truly know what to expect or what it's like to care for a tiny little human. The reality is that until you've looked after a baby before, you'll likely have no idea how to do even the basics of diapering, burping, or even holding them properly. Whether you want to admit it or not, you're likely shaking in your boots. Just remind yourself that there have always been things in your life that you had to learn first in order to get good at it, such as riding a bicycle. I've been in that exact same position. I think it's safe to say that all first-time fathers have. You are, in fact, a "first-time" father. Now, having been through it a few times already, I know you will learn quickly how to do all your new tasks. Yes, the journey to the unknown can be scary but you will get through it the only way anyone can: one step at a time.

- **Failure:** Nobody likes to fail, particularly when you so desperately want to be a good father to your new little one. There will be many times when you'll doubt yourself or even make yourself believe you don't have what it takes to be a good dad. Always remember that as much as you'd like to be one, there is no such thing as a perfect dad. All we as fathers can do is try our best every day, learn from the mistakes that we make, and love our families.

- **Not providing for the family:** I haven't met a single father who didn't want the best for his children. Unfortunately, many people measure this by how many things they can buy for them. I remember when I was dealing with the fear of not being able to provide enough, a good friend told me to just make sure they had food to eat, clothes to wear, and a warm bed to sleep in. As long as they have that, they'll be fine. He also joked that children spell "love" differently to adults. They spell it "T-I-M-E." I reminded myself of that every time I felt bad about not being able to buy them the latest hoverboard or gaming console. When I couldn't afford to splurge, I made up for it by spending quality time with them. That is, after all, another way of providing for your family.

- **Not bonding with your baby:** As I've discussed, your wife started bonding with your baby long before the little one was born. It's only natural that this process will take slightly longer for you. But, never give up, no matter how long it may take to create this bond with them. Spend as much time as you can with your little one and be patient. That magical connection you're seeking will come, and it will be worth the wait, trust me.

STRATEGIES TO OVERCOME ANXIETY

While your "New Dad Anxiety" may be completely normal and even justified, there are many ways to overcome it. There was a time when I wondered if I would ever get myself out of the rut I was in. I was completely overwhelmed by the new life that I had wanted and helped to create. But, it doesn't always have to be this way. Doing research helped me to understand why I was feeling the way I did. What I discovered not only assisted me in finding strategies to overcome my worries but also helped me find joy in fatherhood:

I started opening up: I have always been one of those men who didn't like to talk about my own feelings. After struggling with my mental health as a first-time dad, I realized that this was one of the first areas I would need to work on. I was lucky to have many close friends who were also fathers at different stages of the parenting journey. I realized that I had a network of fellow dads who understood my struggles without judgment and could share tips that had helped them. Even though it was a bit scary in the beginning to become vulnerable in front of them—I couldn't pretend that I had no feelings anymore—I not only gained deeper friendships but I was able to work through my struggles. Well, most of them, any way.

I worked on my sense of humor: No, I don't mean racking up a full supply of dad jokes. Or, maybe I did do a little bit of that too. Instead, developing a solid sense of humor helped me to appreciate funny moments in life. It helped me to laugh when my son smacked me in the face with a baseball bat. Or, when I only realized once I was at work that I forgot to take the nail polish off that my daughter insisted on putting on for me. What's more, it helped me not to be so hard on myself and to live by the mantra that I am doing the absolute best I can.

I practiced self-care: When one of my friends asked me what I was doing just for myself, I couldn't answer him. Especially during the latter part of my wife's pregnancy, my focus was on her and making sure she was okay. Then, after the birth of our firstborn, I tried to help out as much as I could. I was rushing from work every day so I could spend as much time with them to bond and help out. When my friend asked about my self-care, I told him point-blank I wasn't going to be so selfish with my time. He quickly helped me realize that practicing self-care was not a selfish act, but absolutely essential to stay afloat. It's actually selfless, as when you are functioning properly, everyone around you reap the benefits. It's as the old saying goes, "You can't pour from an empty cup." I discussed this with my wife and we agreed on times we would both get a few minutes to ourselves. I believe this helped both of our mental health a great deal.

I became more mindful: When a fellow father first suggested that I should adopt mindful habits, I literally laughed out loud. I didn't have a good perception of mindfulness, simply because I didn't actually understand it. I always thought of mindfulness as a wishy-washy term people used to make excuses for themselves. He explained to me that it's simply a way of consciously directing your focus to the present moment to help you focus on what's truly important. Despite his lengthy explanations, my friend saw I wasn't taking him seriously, so he suggested we do a bet: If I was able to incorporate a specific amount of mindful techniques over a set period of time, I would win the bet and some prize money. And, if I wasn't able to do this, he would win. My competitive streak came out, and I went all in. I won the bet but wouldn't accept the agreed-upon prize money; I couldn't put a price tag on the value I got from becoming more mindful. These are the habits that I'm still practicing today:

- Meditation:

No, my new friends, you don't have to sit on the floor with your legs crossed chanting "ohm" to meditate. You can meditate anywhere and at any time. I tried to go to the quietest place possible (which was mostly before my children woke up). Then, I would settle into a rhythm of deep breathing, and just sit quietly for a few minutes. If any thoughts popped into my head, I would take note and accept them without judgment before returning my focus to my breathing. There are many short five to ten-minute videos available online that will help you learn how to meditate. I do recommend that you start with short meditation sessions, such as five minutes. This way you won't set too high expectations as meditation, like any new skill, is a muscle that needs to be built.

- Journaling:

I always thought of journaling as something teenagers or middle schoolers given a prompt by their teacher do, until I gave it a go. I didn't use a traditional book-type journal but downloaded the Daylio app on my phone that would remind me to jot down my feelings, thoughts, and plans. The algorithms on the app would then determine what specific negative patterns I followed, particularly when it came to my moods, which helped me identify many of my triggers and challenges.

- Exercise:

I've always enjoyed a good workout but with a newborn in the house, it was challenging to find enough time to be active. Or perhaps, lack of time was just my excuse for when I didn't have the energy to go to the gym after not sleeping properly. I had to make the mindset shift to get active again and remind myself that working out doesn't always mean I had to go to the gym. I started doing exercises in and around the house and even incorporated my baby in these activities, such as doing sit-ups while he was lying on my chest or putting him in the stroller for a jog or walk around the park. Babies can be surprisingly great workout toys; my biceps have never been as big as when I used them as weights.

- Eating well:

Life with a newborn didn't do our nutrition any favors; it was just so much easier to order takeout than to cook healthy meals. Unfortunately, all that oil and salt depleted our energy even more. After searching on social media, we found someone in our area who sold healthier frozen meals for those nights we didn't have the time or energy to cook. We also decided to only keep healthy snacks in the house. Although hard at first, these small changes made a massive difference.

- Cold showers:

I've heard many gym fanatics swear by cold showers but I honestly never had the guts to try it, unless it was really hot out. When I researched this, I was amazed at the many benefits it can bring, not just for your physical health but also your mental toughness and boosting your mind-over-matter capabilities. Now, I try to start every shower with warm water and gradually decrease the temperature to as cold as I can handle. You'd be surprised at the energy boost you feel after.

- Sleep better:

While proper sleep might seem like an unattainable dream when you have a newborn in the house, you can make changes to increase your odds of getting the best possible sleep when you get the chance. We worked on making sure we set the right atmosphere in our bedroom, which included adding a blackout blind in front of the window, installing a new air conditioner, and downloading sleep sounds. We also created a rule not to use any screens for up to an hour before we planned on sleeping, as the blue light emitted from these devices can slow down your body's natural release of melatonin, the hormone that helps you fall asleep.

- Partner check-in:

When you're the parents of a newborn, your lives revolve around your baby and making sure all their needs are met. Unfortunately, this can create distance in your relationship with your partner. One of the ways my wife and I worked at overcoming this was to do weekly check-ins. We decided to do this on a Sunday afternoon while the baby was sleeping. During this time, we would briefly talk about our week with a specific focus on what we appreciated about each what we'd like to continue doing. This not only helped us to discuss our relationship but also to focus on the positives with each other. In Chapter 6, we'll discuss more ways of keeping the spark in your intimate relationship alive.

As you've seen, none of these positive habits require a lot of time. Later in this book, we'll go into more detail on how you can steal a few minutes to take care of yourself.

BUILDING CONFIDENCE THROUGH SMALL WINS

When we think of our children and our role in raising them, we tend to think of the big moments. You may think of your baby taking their first steps or wondering whether their first word will be "mama" or "dada." You may already dream about going to your child's first dance recital, basketball game, or teaching them how to ride a bike. Perhaps, you've already started a college fund or savings account for their wedding. While all of these are important milestones in any parent's life, they aren't the only thing that contributes to your overall experience of parenthood. Instead, it's those little things that make it all worthwhile. And, it's also those small wins that boost your confidence and remind you that you're doing a great job.

I distinctly remember the day when the importance of focusing on the positives really kicked in for me. I had to go away for a few days due to work obligations. I never used to mind doing work trips before I became a father, even though I preferred staying at home with my wife. Once I cut that umbilical cord, things were different. As much as there were times when I felt I could do with a break, I never wanted to be away from home for too long. Not only did I not want to let my wife fly solo with the parenting duties but I also feared missing out on important milestones. As a result, I tried my very best to avoid and postpone work trips. Eventually, I ran out of excuses not to go away.

During this five-day trip, many of those traditional big parenting moments happened. My baby said his first word (which, surprisingly, was "dada"), he cut his first tooth, and he took his first step. I missed all of them. I felt like an absolute failure as a father. These were moments I was looking forward to for months and they all happened over a few days while I was out of town. Funny how that timing worked out, huh? My wife did send me videos but it just wasn't the same as actually being there. Naturally, by the time I came home, my son was on his second word ("mama") and I had to wait for more than a week of me continuously saying "dada" before he said it again.

It was at that same time when I so desperately wanted him to call me that I realized hearing him say that magical word wasn't the most important thing. I was sitting on the living room floor one night while he was playing with his noisiest toys. Those are the same toys that I would usually make "Go Houdini" because listening to the same ridiculous tune on repeat isn't exactly my idea of fun. However, after being away for a week, I could bear it again.

I took my eyes off my son for a split second to read an email that had just come through on my phone. The next minute, I felt his tiny hands pushing on my leg. When I looked down, he was busy climbing onto my lap. Once he made his way up, I had two of those small winning moments. First, it was listening to his laugh as he was repeatedly hitting me in the face with a teddy. Then, the biggest small moment of all: He pushed his head into my chest and just sat like that for a few minutes. It was his way of hugging me and at that moment, I couldn't imagine myself being prouder of him and my little family. I realized that missing those traditional important moments was okay since what does matter is the absolute love that lives in my home, despite the chaos we often have to live through.

That night, I decided that I would live more in the moment so that I could really appreciate those small wins in life. This mindset change also helped a lot in calming any "New Dad Anxiety" I still experienced, as I allowed the little moments to motivate me and remind me that even though it didn't always feel like it, I was being the best dad I could possibly be for my child. Celebrating our small wins together strengthened our bond as a family. We grew closer than ever before.

OVERCOME THE FEARS OF FATHERHOOD

While the tips we discussed above may already be enough to reduce your "New Dad Anxiety," you might need to do more, especially if you have very specific fears or triggers to work through. Let's discuss things you can do to overcome some of the most common worries you may face:

- If you worry that you won't be able to provide for your family, you may benefit from consulting with a financial planner to not only help you plan and save for the future but also budget effectively. There are also many free resources online as well as books on how you can earn extra cash, should you wish to go that route.
- If you don't have any friends who are dads, you can consider joining support groups for dads, either in your area or on social media. Also, keep in mind that once your child goes to daycare or school, you're bound to meet other dads who can become good friends in the future.
- If you fear parenthood is negatively affecting your relationship with your partner, it's best to talk to her openly and make plans together on how you can work through these challenges.
- If you fear that you won't be a good father, take some time to think about the type of dad you want to be or what good role models you have in your life

that you might want to emulate. Think about what these fathers do or if you can, ask your role model for advice. Then, consider what you can do to bring you closer to the type of father you want to be.

- If you fear you won't have a strong bond with your baby, spend as much time with them as possible. Take charge of as many of the parenting duties as you can. We'll discuss bonding in more detail in Chapter 3.

If you or a loved one experience prenatal or postpartum anxiety or depression symptoms that intensify or last longer than a few weeks, talk with your doctor about possible treatment options. Always remember there is no shame in admitting that you need help. Instead, it should be seen as a sign of strength and love for your family.

TEST YOUR NEW DAD IQ: CHAPTER 2

Now that we've discussed "New Dad Anxiety," its many potential causes, and how you can overcome it, let's do a quick check to test your new dad IQ. If you struggle with any of these questions, refer back to the various sections in the chapter to refresh your memory.

1. **Is it true that "New Dad Anxiety" affects many first-time dads?**
2. **Can you name some of the common causes of "New Dad Anxiety?"**
3. **Why should self-care be considered a selfless act instead of being selfish?**

4. How can focusing on the small wins help you on your parenting journey?

5. If you fear not being able to provide for your family financially, should you go to the casino and take your chances at winning big?

You're steadily navigating the waters of "New Dad Anxiety," but what about the bond between you and your baby? Let's dive into the magical world of father-child bonding in the next chapter: Dad's Role: Bonding With Your Newborn.

CHAPTER THREE

DAD'S ROLE: BONDING WITH YOUR NEWBORN

Before the birth of our first baby, my wife and I spoke at length about how we wanted to raise our child. Regardless of how he would be born, the plan was always that my wife would do skin-to-skin contact as soon as possible and perhaps try to breastfeed the baby. Then, it would be my turn to hold him.

When it was time for the delivery, everything went close to perfect, until it was my time to hold him. Suddenly, I was a ball of nerves and the clumsiest I've been in my entire life. I've held many babies in my life but at that moment, I was so uncoordinated that I wouldn't be able to catch a giant beach ball (and as a coach in multiple sports who prides myself on my hand-eye coordination, that's saying a lot). I remember the look on my wife's face when she tried to hand our son to me. It was a complete mixture of shock and confusion, perhaps with a touch of disgust mixed in there.

After my wife tried a few times to unsuccessfully hand the baby to me, the delivery nurse intervened. She told me exactly how I should hold my body and placed my son in my arms. I'm not going to pretend that I didn't feel uncoordinated the next few times I tried to pick our son up but eventually, it became second nature. Soon, I was doing my part to bond with our baby.

You see, my new fellow friends, bonding isn't just a maternal thing; it's equally essential for dads. When you create this connection with your new little one, you lay the foundation for your future relationship and allow your baby to feel safe and secure in their daddy's arms. What's more, you're also boosting their brain development, as repeated human contact allows your baby's brain to release the different hormones needed for memory, thought creation, and even language (*Bonding and Attachment: Newborns*, 2018).

Speaking of language, did you know that a newborn can recognize their father's voice from birth and, by three weeks, a baby can visually distinguish their dad's face? So, go right ahead, fellas. Hold your baby, talk to them, stroke their soft skin, and be the loving, awesome, and rockstar dad I know you were destined to become.

DIFFERENT OPTIONS FOR BONDING

Bonding with your little one should start as soon as possible after birth, and within the first hour, both parents should have had the chance to hold the newest member of the family. Many medical professionals refer to these first 60 minutes as the "golden hour," as both you and your baby will be primed to form this bond.

This is also why most healthcare professionals involved in the birth will delay tasks like weighing and measuring your baby until after you and your partner have had time to hold the baby post-birth. Unfortunately, there may be many reasons why you might not be able to hold your baby immediately after they are born. This is particularly the case when there are complications. Should these complications be so severe that your baby has to go to the neonatal intensive care unit (NICU), it may be weeks before you can put your baby on your bare chest.

Speak to the nurses in the NICU about other ways you can connect with your baby. You might be able to hold their hands and feet or touch their head while they are in the incubator. Alternatively, you can talk to them while seated in their vicinity. This way your baby will still sense your presence even if you can't physically hold them.

While skin-to-skin contact has many benefits, as discussed in Chapter 1, let's now look at other ways in which you can bond with your little one. Since you're a first-time dad who might not feel qualified to bond with your baby, here are some suggestions to get you started:

- Respond as quickly as you can when your baby is crying. Many people believe you should teach a young baby to self-soothe or even that you'll spoil the baby if you respond every time they cry. I completely disagree with that; you can't spoil a newborn baby. Also remember, crying is the only way your baby can communicate with you. It's their own, special language. So, when they cry, help them to feel secure by tending to their needs or identifying something that might be wrong.

- Touch, stroke, or cuddle your baby when you can. This will help them to hear your heartbeat, which will make them feel safe. On this note, remember that for the nine months of pregnancy, your baby heard your partner's heartbeat the whole time. Recreating this will feel familiar to them.

- Make lots of eye contact with your baby when you interact with them. Remember to hold your baby close to your face so that they can see you and connect your voice, that they'll know so well already, with your face.

- Apart from talking to your baby, you can also sing to your baby. They won't care that you're not a Grammy award-winning singer or if you mess up the lyrics to the song. Just hearing your voice will be enough for them. Also, the more your baby hears you sing or talk, the quicker their language ability will develop.

Even if you are a super dad in the attentive department and swoop in whenever they need you, it can take some time to properly bond with your little one. For some people, it can take a few weeks or even months before you and your baby will truly understand and know each other. If this is the case, don't put too much pressure on yourself or your baby. Your partner had a nine-month head start, so don't beat yourself up. Apart from spending as much time as possible with them to get to know their different reactions, you can't force the bond. Be patient and enjoy the time you have with your tiny human.

I will never forget the moment when I knew my baby recognized me. It was within the first month. I always tried to talk to and around him as much as I could so that he could learn my voice. I actually started doing this while my wife was still pregnant; I read that babies can hear voices from inside the uterus, so I was willing to give it a go. Every night as I scrolled through news sites on my phone, I would read the articles out loud.

The first week or so after my baby's birth, my wife and I were responding to every sound he made. Until the one day when it was clear he knew me. Yes, sure, he probably didn't know I was his dad, but he knew I was someone important to him and that he should feel safe in my arms. Nothing crazy about that day, as I was just holding him in my arms like I usually do. He had just woken up from a nap and was a little cranky. Shocker! While he was lying in my arms, he looked up at me. He studied my face so intensely like babies all know how to do so well, it felt like he was looking into my soul.

The more he looked at me and heard my voice, the more his whole body started to relax. Something changed in his eyes. He gave me the kind of look that screamed, "Wait a second... I know you!" It was like my face triggered his brain's lost and found department. He stopped crying. I'm not sure how long we sat like that with him looking up at me; a newborn baby's attention span is extremely short, so it probably wasn't long. But, in that magical moment, time stood still.

After that day, the moments when our son recognized us became more frequent. He was about a month old when he would smile at the sight of his parents. Soon after that, he would do proper belly laughs whenever I made funny faces. Fellas, these are heart-melting moments to look forward to and capture, which we'll discuss more in Chapter 7.

VARIOUS WAYS TO HOLD YOUR BABY

In the first chapter, we briefly touched on how to pick your baby up and the importance of always supporting your newborn's neck. My main issue came in how to actually hold my son. I suddenly felt like an octopus with way too many arms flopping around. Once I got the hang of it and gained more confidence in my new father role, picking up and holding my baby quickly became second nature. Soon, you will feel the same.

If you feel as clumsy and uncoordinated as I did when I first had to hold my baby, let's look at the different steps to turn you into a pro:

Step 1: Clean your hands. You should always make sure your hands are clean before you handle your baby. As I've mentioned, a newborn's immune system is still developing, so it's best to wash your hands thoroughly and, if possible, use a hand sanitizer. Also, request all your guests to clean their hands before holding your baby.

Step 2: Make sure you're comfortable. Before you pick your baby up, make sure you have everything you might need ready, especially if you're going to hold your baby for a long time, such as letting them nap in your arms. You might need a pillow to support your arm holding the baby (even though they are tiny, they can feel surprisingly heavy after a while) as well as snacks or water to sip on. Also, if you're planning on cuddling your baby for a while, go to the bathroom beforehand. I've tried to do a toilet trip while holding my sleeping baby in my arms and trust me, it's not as easy as it may seem.

Step 3: Support their bodies. As I've mentioned, you should always support your newborn baby's neck when you pick them up. Also, pay special attention to where the fontanelles (soft spots at the top of your baby's skull) are so that you don't accidentally bump against them.

Step 4: Decide on a position. After you've picked your baby up, you need to decide how you want to hold them. As long as you are supporting their necks and are under their butts, you can hold them in almost any position that feels comfortable and relaxing for you both. Here are some common positions you can try:

- Cradle hold:

This is one of the easiest ways to hold a baby, particularly when they are still very little, as it will free up your other hand to do things. Simply bend your arm and let your baby lie on it, supported by your chest. Your baby's head will be cradled into the crook of your elbow while your hand will support their bottom.

- Shoulder hold:

This position is great for doing skin-to-skin contact as well as burping your baby. Hold your baby in an upright position. Let their head and body rest on your shoulder and chest, almost as if they're looking behind you. If you're sitting back or lying down like this, both your arms can be free. If you're sitting upright, you can use one hand to support their necks, while the other one is supporting their bottom.

- Belly hold:

This hold can be handy when your baby is gassy, has stomach cramps, or even for burping them. Hold your arm out and lay your baby on your forearm with their head toward your elbow. Their legs will hang on either side of your arm. If you want to burp your baby or help them get relief from gassiness, you can gently rub their back either upward or downward.

Ultimately, as long as you don't drop your baby or hold them up by one foot and let their body dangle to the floor, you should be all right.

SHARING RESPONSIBILITIES: PARTNERING WITH YOUR SIGNIFICANT OTHER

In the same way, you need to adjust to caring for your brand-new baby, you and your partner will have to slot into your new roles, not just as parents but also as co-parents. The day you gain the responsibility of becoming a dad, that same day life as you know it will change. While this change can most definitely be for the better, it can take some time to get used to your new life and what is expected of you.

There were many days when I felt completely frustrated with my new reality. I couldn't make my typical stops after work or even do the things I used to enjoy. With a newborn whose immune system is still developing, you naturally want to spend more time at home to keep them safe from germs and bacteria. There were times when I felt like a prisoner in my own home; being closed up like that didn't work well with my extroverted personality. But, the days of struggle were outlasted by the absolute beauty of parenthood. I was amazed by my new family, and the love I experienced every day changed my life, for the absolute better.

Yes, I didn't have the freedom to come and go as I pleased anymore, and yes, I had a lot more worries, anxiety, and responsibilities, but that comes with growing up, as my father once told me. Looking at my baby and seeing what an amazing mother my beautiful wife was, made me forever grateful for the incredible blessings I had. Reminding myself of how lucky I was, made me appreciate my wife more than ever before. This made it easier to find ways of sharing the parenting load.

I wanted to help, not only to make it easier for my partner (because, let's face it, during the pregnancy and childbirth she more than did her part in creating our family), but also to bond with my baby. I only had a few days off at home after my son's birth and wanted to make sure I used this time as much as possible to bond with him. At that time, my wife was still trying to breastfeed so apart from helping with burping, I couldn't do much bonding then. After discussing how we could split our parenting responsibilities more, we decided that bath time would be daddy-son time. I loved having these few minutes alone with our baby which was a dedicated special time. Plus, it gave my wife a few minutes to just be a person and do something else.

Although breastfeeding does result in natural bonding time for your partner and your baby, you can find other times to bond with your little one, like I did with bath time. For example, you can bond while holding your baby or carry them in a sling while you move around the house. After your partner has finished nursing your tiny human, you can join in the fun by burping your baby. Many young babies swallow a lot of air while they're drinking, especially when they don't latch properly. Their digestive systems aren't strong enough to bring the gas up again, so they need help, otherwise these gases can cause them pain or discomfort. To burp your baby, you can either let them sit on your leg while supporting their neck, put them tummy-down on your lap, or let them lie tummy-down on your chest. Then, simply rub their backs in an upward direction to bring the gas up. Many people might suggest that you pat their backs as well. Yes, this does work but the patting motion can break the winds up, which can result in them having more gas to try and help them get rid of it.

However you decide to get involved in your baby's care, create your own rhythm that works for you and your partner. The way in which the two of you co-parent can have a huge impact on your baby. This will be their first taste of teamwork. Creating a peaceful environment where you and your partner support each other, will provide amazing teaching opportunities for your little one. The way you interact with your partner will be an example to your child on how to treat other people with respect and communicate courteously.

Every person's circumstances are different. You and the mother of your baby might not be in a relationship with each other, which can make co-parenting more challenging. But, this doesn't mean you can't still be involved in your child's life and raise them together as a team. If you are both committed to giving your child the love and affection from both parents that they deserve, you can make it work. Depending on the nature of your separated relationship with your former partner, you can discuss visitation arrangements. In cases of severe conflict, it might benefit both of you (and especially your baby) to seek the help of a social worker trained in family matters.

TEST YOUR NEW DAD IQ: CHAPTER 3

Bonding with your baby will help you build a strong connection with them and understand their cues a lot better. This will make it easier for you to tend to their needs. Let's do a quick check to test your new dad IQ. If you struggle with any of these questions, refer back to the various sections in the chapter to refresh your memory.

1. **How long should you wait after your baby has been born before you start bonding with them?**
2. **Why is it important to make eye contact with your baby?**
3. **How can you bond with your baby if your partner is breastfeeding?**
4. **Why should you share parenting responsibilities with your partner?**
5. **Will your baby hate you for singing off-key to them?**

As we unearth the beauty of bonding, we also recognize that the daily grind awaits! As a new dad, you're bound to be hands-on with parenting duties and tasks around the house. Up next, we're diving into how you can tackle day-to-day tasks with finesse and perhaps a touch of fun! Ready to master the daily dad duties?

CHAPTER FOUR

TACKLING DAY-TO-DAY TASKS LIKE A PRO DAD

Caring for a newborn baby will require you to suddenly become an expert at doing things you've never had to do before. You may also have to make peace with the fact that there may constantly be a bit of an odor hanging in the air. My second baby had severe reflux and no matter how much we burped her after every feed or how many burp cloths we used to catch any spit up, we would always end up smelling like sour milk. Even changing into clean clothes didn't help as the odor seemed absorbed by our skin, and there just wasn't time to have a shower after every feed. So, fellas, I had to make peace with sour milk being my new cologne.

The utter truth is that accepting these more nasty aspects of parenthood is just one of the many new dad tasks you'll have to deal with. Soon, you'll find yourself consumed by washing and sterilizing bottles, feeding, burping, and soothing your baby and obsessing over the color, consistency, and frequency of your baby's poop. Yes, my fellow dads, you'll change more diapers than you could imagine. Just in the first year, babies go through about 2,200 diapers (*How Many Diapers Do I Need for a Newborn?* 2020). You could either see this as 2,200 times you'll have to do this monotonous task, or as 2,200 opportunities to shine as a new dad.

Let's dive into some of the everyday tasks every new dad has to do, including diapering, tummy time, soothing your crying baby, helping your baby adopt healthy sleeping patterns, and why creating a routine could save you and your new family from the chaos that parenthood can bring.

DIAPERING BASICS: FROM CHOOSING THE RIGHT DIAPER TO TACKLING DIAPER RASH

From the day you find out you're going to become a dad, you know that you'll have one of the biggest jobs of your life coming your way: changing diapers. I have to be honest with you. This was probably the part of fatherhood that I was least looking forward to. I struggled to even imagine myself doing it but I realized that I didn't have a choice. On some days this wasn't a pretty picture. It took me a few pee shots in the face to realize that I should always keep my son's business closed with either the diaper or a wet wipe to avoid his fountain spraying in all directions. And when messes landed on me, I tried my best to imagine it was some moldy chocolate to avoid hurling all the way to the bathroom (I have a pretty weak stomach).

Just like I could turn myself into a diaper-changing master, you can as well. Let's first look at the very basics of diapering. Before you even attempt to change the diaper, make sure you have all the necessary supplies within reach. The last the you want is to leave your baby alone on the changing table while you get something or carry your half-naked baby around with you and turn your arm into a porter potty. We always kept extra diapers, wet wipes, bum cream, rash cream, and a change in clothing on the changing table.

To change a diaper, simply open it, gently lift your baby's butt, and use a wet wipe, cotton ball, or washcloth to wipe them clean from the front to the back. This is to reduce the spread of bacteria which could easily result in urinary tract infections, particularly in girls. Once your baby is clean, you can place the new diaper and apply either bum cream (to provide a barrier to protect their skin) or rash cream if your baby has a rash. Always wash your hands before and after changing their nappy.

I have to pause here and share a crucial tip that will save you a lot of time, wet wipes, and elbow grease. Your baby's first few poops, called meconium, will be black and extremely sticky. You'll easily use a whole packet of wet wipes to clean it off their skin or destroy a washcloth so badly that you'll have to throw it away. This meconium typically passes within a few days. To avoid struggling to clean the meconium, apply petroleum jelly to their skin instead of the normal bum cream. The meconium then sticks to the jelly and not their skin, making it easy to just wipe clean. Once the meconium has passed, you can use the barrier cream of your choice.

Soon, you'll become the ultimate king at diapering. It's estimated that an average baby uses around 3,000 diapers only in the first year. If you use disposable diapers, this can easily cost you anything from $1,000 to $3,000 a year, depending on the brand you choose to use (Tech Team, 2023). If you factor in the cost of wet wipes and bum cream, caring for your newborn's bottom can really break the bank.

The cost of disposable diapers as well as the impact they have on the environment are two of the main reasons many people opt for cloth diapers. You can get really nice sets of cloth diapers for between $500 to $1,000 which you'll be able to use throughout your diapering journey and reuse should you have another child (Tech Team, 2023). Yes, you'll still have the expense of wet wipes (unless you only use a washcloth) and bum cream, as well as cleaning products for when you wash the diaper. All of this can add up to quite a substantial expense to have upfront. However, if you look at the bigger picture, you will save money if you use cloth diapers.

Dealing With Diaper Rash

Regardless of the type of diaper you use, there will likely come a time when you'll have to deal with a diaper rash. This is a form of dermatitis on the baby's bottom, inner thighs, and genitals that looks red, inflamed, bumpy, itchy, and sore. While there may be many causes for diaper rash, the most common ones include:

- Leaving a diaper that's wet or soiled on for too long.
- Using a diaper that's too small or too tight can result in their skin getting irritated from chaffing and rubbing.
- Applying a new product to your baby's skin or on their clothes, particularly if the product is scented.
- Developing a yeast or bacterial infection which can easily spread in the diaper area that's often warm and moist.
- Introducing new types of foods once your baby starts eating solids results in changes to their stool contents, which can cause rashes when in context with their skin. A breastfed baby can also get a rash from something the mother has consumed.
- Having sensitive skin, particularly if the baby has a dermatological condition, such as atopic dermatitis or seborrheic dermatitis.
- Taking antibiotics can kill the bacteria that control yeast, which can result in an increased risk of rashes.

In most cases, diaper rashes can be treated fairly easily using a topical cream. However, if it hasn't improved after a few days, is accompanied by a rash, bleeds, or oozes, or if your baby is in a lot of pain or discomfort because of it, it's best to consult a health care professional. A doctor will be able to eliminate any dermatological conditions that might have resulted in the rash and prescribe medicine or ointment to treat the rash.

While it may be inevitable that your child may develop a diaper rash at some point, there are many things you can do to prevent it:

- Change their diaper frequently and as soon as you can after they soiled it. If your child is in daycare, it would be smart to ask the staff to change their diaper more frequently.
- Rinse your baby's bum with warm water at every diaper change. While wet wipes and a washcloth can help to clean their bums, this may cause pain when you wipe over their irritated and inflamed skin. Gently pat dry their skin or let them air dry.
- Make sure you don't secure the diaper too tightly. Slight airflow between the diaper and the skin can help to reduce any irritation in the area.
- Give your baby a few hours without a diaper on. Exposing their sensitive skin to air can help to dry properly. If you're scared your baby will make a toileting mess while they are diaper-free, you can put them on a large towel for a safe home base.
- Always make sure you use enough bum or barrier cream after every diaper change to make sure their skin is protected. There are also many creams you can buy over the counter to treat a diaper rash. Alternatively, you can try these natural remedies:

  - *Apply coconut oil straight to your baby's clean, dry skin after every use. Coconuts have antimicrobial properties which can not only help to heal a wound but also act as barrier protection.*

- *If your partner is breastfeeding, you can drop some breast milk straight onto the inflamed skin of your child. Allow the area to dry before you put their diaper back on.*
- *Diaper creams with zinc oxide or olive oil can be extremely effective in treating irritations to the skin, as these natural ingredients aid in reducing the burn in the skin. These types of creams can be used on any skin type, including very sensitive skin.*

Perhaps most importantly, always keep an open mind when you're diapering. I will never forget the day when my baby made such a big explosion in his diaper that I never thought I would be able to clean the mess (or get the smell out of my nose). To make matters worse, I was holding him when the poop started leaking out of his diaper, resulting in my arm and chest getting soaked as well. While I was wiping and wiping to get it all cleaned (I eventually resorted to putting us both in the bath), I burst out in laughter. I could either find the funny in the situation, or I could sit in a smelly heap of self-pity. I chose to find the humor.

THE MAGIC OF TUMMY TIME

During the first few weeks, your newborn will only be awake for a few minutes at a time in between naps. These will mostly be spent feeding, burping, diapering, and then soothing your baby before they fall asleep again. Soon, this will change. Over the following few weeks, they will be awake for longer periods of time and start to engage more, not just with you but with toys as well. Now would be time for the introduction of tummy time.

Tummy time simply refers to placing your baby on their stomach when they are awake while keeping a watchful eye to make sure they don't choke on anything or injure themselves. Tummy time holds many benefits for your baby:

- Your baby's back, neck, shoulder, and arm muscles will strengthen, which will help them to sit independently, crawl, or walk over the coming months.
- Your baby will become more coordinated in their movements as their motor skills develop.
- You'll prevent any flat spots at the back of your baby's head, which is a common occurrence in babies who spend most of their time lying on their backs.

Most babies can start tummy time within the first few days of being born. When they are so young, it's best to keep these sessions short as your baby will tire very quickly. It's best to do these sessions during a time when your baby is happy and content. Around three to five minutes at a time will be more than long enough. As they grow, you can push it to slightly longer sessions repeated a few times during the day. These tips can help make tummy time fun and easy for you and your baby:

- Put a soft blanket on the floor.
- Roll a towel up or use a small round pillow. Prop this under your baby's arms to help them into a slightly more upright position and take the strain off their core muscles.
- Put a toy or something with clear patterns in front of them to keep them engaged, or lie on your tummy in front of your baby with your face close to theirs.

It may be best to avoid doing tummy time straight after a feed as your baby might be uncomfortable due to swallowed winds or too sleepy to properly engage in this exercise. While many babies are happy doing tummy time and even enjoy it, others might dislike it and get cranky. If this is the case for your baby, you can make this time more fun by putting them in different positions or bringing more toys to keep them entertained. Also, keeping these sessions short when they are cranky can help ease your baby into it. Let's look at some age-related tips on introducing tummy time for your baby.

Newborn to 6 Weeks

During the first few weeks, you can incorporate these techniques:

- Instead of putting your baby on the floor, you can lie on your back and put your baby's tummy down on your chest. This way, they can clearly see your face and hear your voice when they lift their little heads.

- Let your baby lie tummy down on your two forearms and walk them through the house.
- Using black and white patterns can help to keep your baby engaged as their limited eyesight can clearly differentiate between dark and light. It's best to keep these patterns 8–12 inches away from their face so that they can clearly see them.
- Place your baby down on their tummy on a yoga or birthing ball. The movement on this ball can help to soothe them if they are cranky or don't enjoy tummy time. Just always make sure that you keep the ball steady and hold your baby the whole time they are on the ball to make sure they don't slip off.

6 to 12 weeks

Once they are getting comfortable with tummy time, you can transition these sessions using the below techniques:

- Experiment with different textures. You can either put your baby down on a textured blanket or use different materials to entertain your baby by gently wiping over their face. This can also help to distract them if they don't enjoy tummy time.
- Place wrist rattles around your baby's arms, and gently put their arms out in front of them. The noise of the rattles will keep their attention in front, which will help them into the optimal position to gain the maximum benefits out of tummy time.

- Hold out a rattle in front of them and shake it until your baby focuses on it. Then, slowly move the rattle around to let your baby's gaze follow the toy. As they get older, your baby will try to grab the toy (speaking from experience).
- Baby gyms can be a great tool to use during tummy time as there will be different colors to look at, music to keep them engaged, and textures to touch.

3 to 4 Months

As your baby gets stronger, they start to lift and keep their heads up by themselves, you can incorporate these techniques:

- Water mats can be a great tool to use during tummy time. These mats are soft for your baby to lie on and contain many floating shapes your baby can watch and try to grab.
- Placing a mirror in front of your baby can be another great way of entertaining and distracting them during tummy time. Even if they don't know that they're looking at themselves, they will have a lot of fun with their new "friend" in the mirror.

4 Months and Older

By now, your baby should be able to keep their heads up independently and reach for objects. These techniques can make tummy time fun:

- Place a tray with different objects on the floor in front of them. These objects can include anything from household items such as sponges or wooden spoons to toys and plastic teething necklaces. Just make sure they are all safe for your baby and don't have any small pieces that can be choked on.
- Put a shallow plastic bowl with some water in front of your baby, add a rubber duck and some friends, and you have a makeshift baby bath. Your baby will enjoy playing with their new floaty friends. Expect to be in a splash zone. If you don't want your carpets or floors to get wet, you might want to do this one outside on a warm day or place a waterproof sheet or even a tarp or trash bag underneath your baby.
- Play games with your baby while they are doing tummy time. Peekaboo is always a fantastic option as it can not only help them enjoy this time but also allow them to understand that even when they can't see you, you'll always be there.

As I've mentioned, these tummy time activities can be great in preventing flat spots on your baby's head, which typically happen when they spend a lot of time lying down. While in most cases this isn't a cause of concern and their heads typically return to a normal round shape as they get older, it is still best to prevent it. If their tummy time isn't enough and the shape of their head still looks slightly like they are from an alien movie, you can incorporate these steps:

- Hold your baby upright as much as possible when they are awake.
- Limit the amount of time your baby spends sitting or lying against something.
- Change your baby's sleeping position in their crib frequently. For example, swap the direction of their bodies around.
- Move your baby's crib to a different spot in their room. That way, they will move their heads in different directions when looking around.

If you're ever worried about your baby's progress during tummy time, their upper body strength, or the shape of their head, it's best to speak to their pediatrician. Even though it will be years before they'll deadlift weights, it's best to be aware of any developmental issues sooner rather than later.

SOOTHING TECHNIQUES FOR A FUSSY BABY: SWADDLING, WHITE NOISE, AND MORE

There's nothing as frustrating as when your baby cries and you have no idea what to do to calm them down. Unfortunately, as much as you may be a pro at bonding with your baby and following their prompts, there still may be times when nothing you try helps to stop the tears from rolling down your little one's cheeks. Or perhaps, bonding hasn't gone as well as you hoped and you still haven't gotten the hang of their different cries yet.

When your baby appears inconsolable, I recommend you follow this checklist to try to bring your baby (and your ears) the comfort they desperately seek:

- Is your baby hungry? When last did they feed?
- Is your baby tired? When are they due for another nap?
- Does your baby have a dirty diaper?
- When last did your baby make a poop? What was the consistency like?
- Does your baby have gas?
- Is your baby struggling with cramps?
- Does your baby have a fever or appear to be sick?
- Is your baby dressed appropriately?
- Is your baby over or under-stimulated?

In most instances, ticking off this list will help you solve their struggles. Unfortunately, there are times when none of these reasons are the culprit, and changing their diaper or feeding them just won't stop the seemingly endless supply of tears. My wife and I found these techniques to be helpful; if not to calm our crying baby, then to calm ourselves. These include:

- Newborn babies have no other way to communicate than to cry, so you can and should expect crying. Also, if you try to see the bigger picture and remind yourself that your baby is trying to communicate something important to you. Those crying sounds at 2 in the morning can become more bearable.

- Give your baby a calming massage by rubbing body lotion onto their skin in slow, circular movements. A warm bath can also help them calm down. Then, spread a swaddling or receiving blanket out so that it forms a diamond shape and fold the top corner in. Lay your baby on the blanket with their head at the folded corner. Either gently cross your baby's arms over their chest or let their arms lie on their sides. Then, wrap the right corner over your baby and tuck it in underneath them. Bring the bottom corner of the blanket over their feet. Lastly, bring the left corner over to complete the swaddle. Always make sure that you wrap them snuggly but never too tight as this can result in hip dislocation or dysplasia.
- Gently rock your baby in your arms, either sitting in a rocking chair or walking up and down with them. If you have a vibrating or rocking chair, these can be very helpful to soothe a crying baby. Many babies are also comforted by the vibration of a moving car, so if all else fails, strap your baby in their car seat, take them for a ride, and pick up drive-through takeout while on the road. Your partner will be happy for the break, especially when neither of you have to cook dinner.
- If none of these tips help, consider getting some help. There will likely be a grandparent, aunt, or uncle who will be more than happy to sit with your baby while you and your partner have a quick break. Perhaps, they may even bring a new approach to soothing your little one that you haven't

tried yet. Even just a few hours away from your little one can be enough to revive you for your next daddy duty shift.

- Should you not have anyone you trust to look after your baby for a few minutes, make sure your baby is placed in a safe environment, such as in their crib or stroller, and leave the room for a few minutes, even if it's just to have a sip of water or make yourself a cup of coffee.

- Before your partner gave birth, or perhaps even during labor, she likely learned some deep breathing exercises to keep her calm. These same breathing exercises can be just as handy when you try to stay calm while your baby is crying. When you hold your baby while you do these deep breathing techniques, they may even pick up on your lowering heart rate.

- If you keep your physical body as healthy as possible, your emotional strength will also improve, which will help you to stay calm. I know it may sound like an old wives' tale to sleep when your baby is sleeping but if it's at all possible (which might be difficult if you're working), try to nap as much as you can during the day. Also, try your best to eat healthy meals. While takeout or processed meals that you only need to heat up may be the easiest and quickest options, healthy meals will help to improve your emotional health.

- You may be hesitant to venture out of the house when your baby is difficult to soothe. However, if you imprison yourself in your house, your frustration levels will likely rise, especially if you're used to having an active social life. Yes, it may be uncomfortable being out and about while your baby is crying and you may even get a few unpleasant looks, but get over this and enjoy the fresh air outside of your home as both of you will benefit.

- The more time you spend with your baby, the more you'll be able to anticipate their needs and pinpoint times in the day when they might be more cranky. This can help you to prepare and deal with their crying more effectively.

Always remember the bigger picture. Right now, you might struggle to see the light outside this crying tunnel but this crying phase won't last forever.

NEWBORN SLEEP PATTERNS: UNDERSTANDING AND ADAPTING

The first few weeks of having a newborn can be rough on a person. While you love that little human you've created with all your heart, caring for them can be exhausting, to say the least. You'll wake up every few hours to feed your baby, burp them, change their diaper, and then help them to fall back asleep. Especially if your baby is breastfeeding and needs to nurse every two hours, you'll just start to fall asleep again before it's time for the next feed. If you're back at work, this can make it difficult to focus. If your partner is alone at home with the baby all day or perhaps also back at work, she will be equally as tired and in need of your help.

You likely can't wait for the day your baby will sleep through the night. For some lucky parents, this can happen as soon as around the six-week mark, whereas for others, it can be months. We had those opposites in our home. Our first baby was just over six weeks old when he started sleeping through the night. We thought we were parents extraordinaire, which gave us confidence for having a second baby. Unfortunately, sleeping luck wasn't on our side the second time around, as this baby only started to sleep through the night at the age of around three years. As bad as it sounds, you do surprisingly get used to not sleeping properly and find ways to cope.

Since every child's sleeping habits can be vastly different, it can be difficult to know what to expect or what is typical for their specific age. Let's look at the typical sleeping needs of a baby over the first year (Pacheco & Wright, 2023):

- **First 4 months:** Newborns typically sleep anywhere between 16 to 19 hours every day. As we've mentioned, this will unfortunately be broken up into short cycles of sleep in between nursing and diaper changes. Since young babies' blood sugar can drop quickly if they don't feed often enough, you'll need to wake them up if they're still sleeping by the time they are due for their next feed. If they gain an acceptable amount of weight by the time they are six weeks old, their pediatrician may give you the green light to leave your little one for longer periods during the night.

- **Months 4 to 6:** During these months, your baby will need between 12 to 16 hours of sleep at a time. They will be able to go longer between feeds, so their sleep will be clustered into longer sleeping cycles. This can mean they'll have between two to three good naps during the day.
- **Months 6 to 12:** Once your baby passes the six-month mark, they should do most of their sleeping during the night. However, there will still be times when they don't sleep well, particularly when they go through growth spurts or are teething.

Always remember every baby develops differently, and so will their sleeping habits. Use the above simply as a guideline and should you ever be in doubt, discuss this with your baby's doctor.

Even if you have your baby on a strict routine (this can help with improving their sleep cycles), you should keep an eye out for their typical sleep cues and when they appear to be tired. Even if it isn't time for a nap, you should consider listening to your baby's needs. These typical sleeping cues can include yawning, rubbing their eyes, fussing, and crying.

Many babies confuse their nights and days. They'll sleep soundly during the day but struggle to settle at night when you desperately want to get some sleep. If you want to create good sleeping habits and create a healthy circadian rhythm (our body's internal clock that regulates time for sleep and alertness), it's best to first make sure they are stimulated during the day and get plenty of daylight. When you need to change or feed them at night, keep the room as dark as you can. Additionally, try to also make their room darker during the day when they need to nap. Over time, they will associate darkness with sleep, which will help you a great deal in also getting some rest.

You can also create good habits to help them settle at night. Some of these habits we introduced include:

- Bathing the baby at night.
- Changing them into their pajamas.
- Putting on a fresh diaper.
- Reading them a story.
- Singing a lullaby.
- Giving them a nighttime feed as late as you can.
- Dimming the lights.
- Making sure the thermostat is at a comfortable temperature.
- Creating a quiet environment.
- Gently rocking them to sleep or putting them in their crib to settle.

If you want to cuddle them while they fall asleep, you can consider rocking and holding them until they are almost asleep before you put them in their crib. Gradually aim at putting them in their crib while they are less sleepy. This way they'll get used to being in their crib and falling asleep, as well as settling themselves back to sleep when they wake up in the night.

Always place your baby on their backs when you put them to sleep as this reduces the risk of sudden infant death syndrome, a condition where babies die in their sleep without any specific reason. If you ever worry about your baby's sleeping habits or if they continue to wake up often during the night despite your continuous efforts to create a healthy circadian rhythm, you may want to discuss this with their pediatrician or even get the help of a sleeping expert. They might give suggestions on things to try or their doctor may prescribe melatonin pills that you can crush and put in your baby's nighttime bottle to help them settle into a healthy sleeping routine. Always consult your pediatrician before you give your baby any medication as some can be extremely harmful, especially within the first three months.

CREATING ROUTINES FOR YOU AND YOUR BABY

Now, let's take a look at the impact of a routine. When my wife first suggested that we create a routine for our baby, I was severely opposed to it. I didn't like the idea of a schedule telling me when I should do something or raising my child on one. However, as the saying goes, "happy wife, happy life." A few hours later we had a full-on schedule and a few weeks later, I was hooked. We kept the schedule fairly basic but included specific times we'd want to bath our son, feed him, and put him to bed. This not only helped us to adapt to our roles but the predictability also helped my son to settle at night when it was time for bed. However, we did remain flexible on days when our baby was difficult. Life happens, especially with a newborn, and it's important to allow you and your partner some flexibility when it does.

If you want to create your own schedule, you should consider your child's feeding times and adjust their routine as they're able to go longer between feeds. We found it's best to start by working around what they are currently happy with when it comes to eating, sleeping, and alert times. Take a few days and make notes of these times so that you can better understand your baby's patterns, which can be helpful in creating a routine.

When you decide to alter their existing routine, it's best to do this gradually so that you don't suddenly spring big changes on them. For example, if you'd like your baby to nap, you can put them down in their crib a little later and increase this daily until you've stretched them to the new nap time. You essentially need to wean your baby into the routine. Also, be mindful that growth spurts can mess with even the best schedules. Your baby may suddenly not want to sleep even though they've been following the same routine for weeks, or they might want to feed a lot more. While following a routine is helpful, you should always be flexible and just hang in there.

You should adjust your baby's schedule as they grow older. Their sleeping and feeding needs will change, particularly when they start eating solids at around six months. They will also spend a lot more time awake and by the time they reach their first birthday, they might only need one or two naps a day.

TEST YOUR NEW DAD IQ: CHAPTER 4

Becoming a master of the various parenting tasks will require you to do the same thing over and over. Just like from the *Karate Kid*: wax on, wax off. Repetition builds discipline and, therefore, builds habits. Eventually, you will get the hang of it and change diapers without giving it any thought. With this in mind, let's do a quick check to test your new dad's IQ. If you struggle with any of these questions, refer back to the various sections in the chapter to refresh your memory.

1. **How long should you wait before you start your baby with tummy time?**
2. **How can you prevent diaper rashes?**
3. **Why is swaddling soothing for your baby?**
4. **How can a routine help you and your baby settle into your new life?**
5. **When your baby has a diaper explosion, should you take them outside and hose them down to clean?**

You're now equipped to tackle daily tasks with what I like to call "rockin' dad energy." Yes, you might cringe at my dad joke here, but guess what, you'll soon be whipping out these dad jokes all the time! It's equally important to be prepared for unexpected health concerns. In our next chapter, we delve deep into navigating complex health issues, ensuring your baby is always in the safest hands: yours.

CHAPTER FIVE

NEWBORN HEALTH GUIDE FOR DADS

Having a sick baby or one with serious health issues is most likely every parent's worst nightmare. I know it was definitely mine. My wife had to stop me from rushing to the doctor whenever my newborn just sneezed. My biggest fear was always febrile convulsions, or fever fits, as most people call it. Unfortunately, that fear became a reality for us.

My son was a few weeks short of his first birthday when my wife got a call from his daycare. They said he didn't look sick and had no fever but something seemed off. He just wasn't his usual, happy self. After fetching him, I insisted that my wife take him to the pediatrician for a checkup, just in case. Apart from a slight rash on his tummy (that only the doctor could see, not us) that we should keep an eye on, the doctor couldn't find any cause for concern.

Just over an hour after getting home, my son started a slight fever. We immediately gave him medication (paracetamol or ibuprofen) to try to break the fever but it didn't work. His fever continued to climb and did so extremely quickly. I started to undress our baby to try to cool him down while we were discussing whether we should go to the emergency room and give it a few more minutes. In the middle of talking about it, suddenly, my son's entire body began to shake. He was having a seizure.

The seizure lasted for less than a minute, although it felt like hours. When it was over, we immediately loaded him in the car and rushed him to the pediatrician. We couldn't believe our eyes when the doctor examined him and we saw the super slight rash from the afternoon, which was now dark red and obvious. The doctor then confirmed that our baby has Roseola—or baby measles—and that febrile convulsions are common due to the rapidly rising fevers that are typical of this disease.

Even though taking our son to the doctor during the afternoon didn't stop his seizure, having gone to the doctor earlier helped the specialist make a diagnosis and start treatment quickly. That day I realized that as parents, and especially new parents, we should always trust our instincts, especially when it comes to the health of our little ones.

To help you navigate your health fears, we'll now look at some of the most common ailments many newborns struggle with, including colic. We'll also discuss whether babies need to take additional vitamins, as well as developmental red flags that should urge you to visit your baby's pediatrician.

COMMON FIRST-NONTH HEALTH CHALLENGES

When you're a first-time dad, any form of health issues can seem extremely daunting, no matter how small and insignificant they may actually be. Unless you have medical training, this may be the first time you're responsible for keeping another human being healthy, which in itself, can feel scary. Luckily, many of the common health challenges many newborns face can be treated easily at home.

Cradle Cap

This is the baby version of seborrheic dermatitis, which results in dandruff in adults (Gill, 2023). In babies, this can result in flaky skin on the baby's scalp and ears, but can sometimes spread to the eyebrows, nose, and armpits as well. While it may look terrifying, it's typically harmless and usually goes away by itself, often by the time the baby reaches three months.

You can follow these three steps to treat cradle cap at home:

- Brush your baby's scalp daily to remove loose flakes of skin from their heads. However, never try to pick on it or scrape it off. You can buy a special brush that's made for cradle caps or a new toothbrush with soft bristles can work just as well. If you see your baby's scalp get agitated, you should brush less often.

- After you've brushed their scalp, you should hydrate it. You can use baby oil or a pure plant oil such as olive, coconut, or almond. Pour a small amount of this oil into your hand and gently massage it into your baby's head, making sure you are extra careful close to their fontanelle, the soft spot on the top of their head. Let the oil soak for a few minutes and wash it off with a fragrance-free baby shampoo.
- If these steps aren't effective, you can ask your doctor to prescribe a cream. They may opt for either an anti-fungal, zinc, or hydrocortisone cream.

Eczema

This skin condition, also known as atopic dermatitis, can affect people of all ages, including newborns. When this happens, the skin will appear chapped. On light skin tones, it can present as red, brown, or purple, and gray on darker skin. Your pediatrician can prescribe a cream to use, or you can try one of these natural remedies:

- Aloe vera gel is regarded as safe to use on an infant's skin and due to its antibacterial and antimicrobial properties, it can soothe eczema.
- Coconut oil can moisturize the skin, which can help to reduce inflammation and soothe eczema.
- Honey has amazing anti-inflammatory and antibacterial properties and can not only help prevent infections in the skin but also speed up healing.

Jaundice

This happens when there is an excess of bilirubin, which is the yellow pigment that can be found in red blood cells. It results in a yellow discoloration of the baby's eyes and skin. It typically happens in babies born prematurely or whose liver hasn't matured enough yet. In most instances of jaundice, babies don't require specialized treatment. However, in severe cases, it can result in brain damage, so it's always best to get an expert medical opinion.

To test if your baby has jaundice, press gently with your finger on your baby's nose or forehead. If the skin changes to a yellow color before returning to its natural color, they may have jaundice. Unless the jaundice is severe, ensuring your baby is exposed to sunlight is usually effective in treating the condition. Dress your baby in only a diaper and sit with them in a sunny spot in your home, ideally with lace curtains drawn to ensure they don't get too hot or sunburnt.

Baby Acne

This results in small pimple-like bumps on your baby's skin, particularly on their face, neck, and back. They are typically caused by an excess of the mom's hormones that are still in the baby's body after the birth. Although they might not look nice, they will typically clear within the first month or two and very seldom leave any scarring.

Although they don't require any treatment, using aqueous cream instead of soap when you bath the baby can help to moisturize the skin and reduce the appearance of these bumps. Unless the bumps become severe or cause your baby discomfort, you shouldn't need to take them to the doctor for baby acne.

Ear Infection

Earache and infections in a baby can be challenging to deal with, particularly since your baby can't tell you that their ears are sore. Your baby will likely cry a lot, particularly when they are feeding or lying down, and their pain might be worse at night. Older babies may move their hands toward their ears. You can test if your baby has earache by gently pressing the tragus of the ear (the triangular piece in the front of the external ear) back to close the ear opening. If your baby's cries intensify as you do this, you can know that their ears are sore.

Since the aches can be caused by an infection, either viral or bacterial, it's best to take your baby to the doctor as they might need antibiotic ear drops to clear the infection. Until the pain subsides, you should take extra caution when you bathe them to keep their ears dry. You can also hold your baby at a slightly upward angle when you feed them.

Reflux

Reflux typically starts within the first few weeks after the baby is born and is usually the result of an underdeveloped esophagus, which causes the milk they drink to push back up. Babies with reflux will bring the milk up either during or shortly after feeding, hiccup during feeds, cry more during and after feeds, and gulp after burping. It may be that your baby shows all the signs of reflux without the typical spit-up or vomit. If this is the case, your baby may have silent reflux.

If you suspect your baby has reflux, it's best to consult their doctor as there are medications you can give to ease their discomfort. If your baby is formula-fed, the doctor might recommend you swap to an anti-reflux milk or even add a special powder to their milk to make it thicker. You can also burp your baby more frequently and for longer after feeds, and keep them upright for a while after burping them. It can help to give your baby smaller bottles of milk more often.

Fevers

It's highly unlikely that you won't ever have to deal with fevers during your parenting journey. Your baby will have a fever if their core temperature rises above 100.4 °F (Pitone, 2022). As scary as fevers may be, they are signs that your baby's body is trying to fight off an infection and unless these fevers reach dangerously high levels or rise rapidly (as was the case with my baby when he got the seizure) they shouldn't necessarily be viewed in a negative light.

Apart from infections, fevers can also be caused by immunizations and even dressing your baby too warm when it's hot out. Teething can also raise a baby's body temperature but should never go higher than 100 °F (Pitone, 2022).

Paracetamol and ibuprofen can be very effective in lowering a fever. However, you shouldn't give a young baby these medicines without checking with their doctor first. You can also lower their body temperature by removing a layer of their clothes and using a lukewarm facecloth to cool them down. Many people recommend a lukewarm sponge bath as well. Even though this can be very effective, it can cause your baby to shiver and be highly uncomfortable. When your baby has a fever, it's important to make sure they stay hydrated as it can result in your baby losing fluids faster than usual.

If your baby's fontanelles are ever sunken in or building outward, or if they vomit repeatedly, struggle to wake up, have purple spots on their skin, bluish lips, tongue, or nails, or get seizures, it's best to take your baby to the emergency room immediately.

Oral Thrush

This yeast infection is another condition that's very common among babies as they lack the immune system to fight off the excess yeast in their bodies. As the name suggests, the signs of oral thrush will all be in and around their mouth: They may have cracks in the corner of their mouths or cottage cheese-like patches on the tongue, lips, or the insides of their cheeks. While most babies won't experience any discomfort, others may struggle to feed well.

In many cases, the infection will go away by itself within a week or two. However, if your baby is struggling to feed, their doctor may recommend an anti-fungal solution to use in the affected areas. You can also take steps to prevent oral thrush in your baby. This will depend on how you feed them:

- **Formula:** Make sure you clean the bottle teats thoroughly by using hot water, and dish soap. Then, sterilize them to make sure you remove any yeast or bacteria. If you prepare the bottles in advance, you should store them in the fridge to prevent yeast from growing in them. If your baby uses a pacifier, you should take these same steps to clean it.

- **Breast:** If your partner's nipples are red or sore, she might have thrush there, which she can pass onto the baby. There are many anti-fungal creams available that she can apply to her breasts to kill the yeast buildup.

SURVIVING THE TERROR THAT COLIC CAN BRING

I have the utmost respect and sympathy for parents of babies with colic. Imagine your baby crying every day for hours on end and absolutely nothing you do can calm them. You go through your checklist to try to find the cause of their unhappiness, you swaddle them, you rock them until you have no feeling left in your arms, you even take them for hours in your car, but their crying just won't end.

Eventually, you take them to the doctor, because surely there must be something wrong with your little one to cause this extreme level of unhappiness. But, after a thorough examination, the doctor says the words you've been fearing: You are the unlucky winner of a baby with colic. The good news is that colic won't last forever. But, the bad news is that it can take up to six months for the colic to gradually go away.

If you're wondering what colic is or what causes colic, you're not alone. Despite extensive research done on the condition, no one has found conclusive reasons why perfectly healthy babies would have these crying spells. A baby is usually considered to have colic when a baby cries for more than three hours a day, for three or more days a week. These crying spells typically happen at the same time of the day, most often in the early evening.

Unfortunately, there isn't a lot you can do to soothe a baby with colic. You can go through the checklist for soothing your crying baby (as discussed in Chapter 4) just to always make sure there isn't an actual reason for them crying. If none of your usual tricks help to soothe your baby, your main focus should be on trying to keep yourself calm. If you can't handle it anymore, put your baby in a safe spot, such as their crib, while you take a few minute's break. Just make sure there are no loose blankets of stuffed animals that can pose a choking or suffocation risk for your little one.

WHICH VITAMINS YOUR BABY MAY NEED

You may wonder whether your baby needs to get additional vitamins to help boost their health. The answer to this question largely depends on the type of milk you choose to feed your baby. While breastmilk is a rich source of nutrients, vitamins, and minerals, it may lack two important nutrients: vitamin D and Iron. However, this will largely depend on the mother's diet while she is breastfeeding and how many foods rich in these nutrients she eats, plus how many her body absorbs before it's passed to her milk.

Vitamin D is predominantly absorbed through sunlight, so if you're worried that your baby isn't getting enough of this vitamin, you can let them lie in the sun for a few minutes a day. Just make sure you have lace curtains to block out harmful rays and avoid their sensitive skin getting sunburnt.

You can also get a liquid vitamin D supplement at your local pharmacy that's safe to give to a baby over the age of three months. Many of these supplements are also rich in vitamins A and C, which not only help with the absorption of vitamin D but iron as well.

Iron is important for healthy brain development. If you suspect your breastfed baby has an iron deficiency, your partner can increase the iron-rich foods she eats, such as leafy green vegetables and meat. Alternatively, you can discuss this with your doctor to get recommendations on an iron supplement to give to your baby.

Supplemental vitamins are typically not necessary for babies who are formula-fed, as their formula will already be fortified with sufficient levels of iron, vitamin D, and many other nutrients. It may be helpful to check the content of these vitamins in your child's formula, or if you're alternating between breast milk and formula, you should discuss any concerns with their pediatrician. Once your baby starts solids at around six months, especially if they are a picky eater, it's best to reconsider their vitamin needs again.

Should you opt to give your baby supplemental vitamins, it's best not to mix them in your baby's milk as the calcium in the milk can affect the absorption of the vitamins, particularly iron.

HEALTH RED FLAG CHECKLIST

Every baby develops at their own pace and, as a result, you should always read the various monthly milestones that are available online with a whole bag of salt (a pinch just isn't enough). With all due respect to these references, they often work on the ideal baby's development, which can be very far removed from reality. Let me give you an example: My eldest developed at a textbook pace: He sat independently at six months, crawled at eight months, and walked just before his first birthday. Then, my wife gave birth to our pocket rocket second child who defied all those typical milestones: She sat independently at four months, crawled at six months, and was literally running around the house at nine months (it seemed like she completely skipped past the walking phase).

Because of my experience, I don't believe in lists of milestones babies should reach by specific months. Instead, I want to share a checklist of red flags that might indicate that it may be a good idea to take your baby to their pediatrician for a checkup (*Red Flags by Age for Referral of a Child*, 2021):

1 month:

- Can't follow moving objects with their eyes, even extremely briefly.
- Doesn't startle when they hear a loud noise.

2 months:

- Doesn't respond to loud noises at all.
- Can't hold their head up during tummy time.

- Can't bring their hands to their mouth.

3 months:

- Can't push their chest up during tummy time.
- Don't turn their head in response to movement.
- Doesn't smile at people.
- Don't laugh when you try to entertain them.

4 months:

- Can't support their own head.
- Doesn't make any coos or sounds.
- Struggles to move their eyes in different directions.
- Don't push down with their legs when you put their feet on a hard surface.

6 months:

- Doesn't reach for things.
- Doesn't respond to sounds.
- Doesn't seem sturdy, almost like a rag doll, or extremely stiff.
- Can't roll over when lying on their backs.
- Shows no affection for others, particularly their primary caregivers.
- Doesn't make sounds, especially vowel sounds.

9 months:

- Can't bear weight on their legs with support.
- Can't sit, even with help.
- Doesn't respond to their own name.
- Can't recognize familiar faces.
- Can't transfer toys from one hand to the other.
- Doesn't look where you're pointing.

12 months:

- Doesn't crawl.
- Doesn't stand with support.
- Doesn't point to things.
- Don't wave bye-bye.
- Doesn't shake their head when they don't want something.
- Doesn't say a single word.
- Loses skills they used to be able to do.

While these red flags don't necessarily mean that there's something wrong with your baby, it's best to have your little one checked out by the doctor to make sure there isn't a medical reason for their slow development.

TEST YOUR NEW DAD IQ: CHAPTER 5

Having a baby with health concerns can be a major worry for all parents, particularly first-time parents who aren't used to caring for the health of another person. Many of the common ailments many newborns face are luckily not serious. Let's do a quick check to test your new dad's IQ. If you struggle with any of these questions, refer back to the various sections in the chapter to refresh your memory on this very important chapter.

1. How can you treat mild cases of jaundice at home?
2. Is colic a result of a medical condition or illness?
3. If your baby has baby acne, does that mean your child will struggle with pimples throughout their childhood into their teenage years?
4. Why shouldn't you add vitamins to a baby's milk?
5. If you have a colic baby, is it okay to put earplugs in your ears and ignore them for hours at a time?

Now that you're equipped with the knowledge to navigate complex health concerns, the journey doesn't stop there. As a new dad, balancing fatherhood with personal life can be a tightrope walk. In the next chapter, let's explore how to find that equilibrium, ensuring you don't lose sight of yourself while embracing your new role.

CHAPTER SIX

BALANCING FATHERHOOD WITH PERSONAL LIFE

I'll never forget one team-building day I had at work. This was a few months after I became a dad for the second time. My colleagues and I did many different activities together. Some were physical (obstacle courses and such), while others were mental and even emotional.

During one of the more mental challenges, we had to answer a series of questions about ourselves. They were mostly easy ones, such as describing yourself in five words, your favorite food, and your dream vacation spot. Those types of questions. However, one of these questions had me completely stumped. We had to jot down our biggest strengths and weaknesses. One answer for each of them, but we only had five seconds to do so. It was one of those moments where you just write down the first thing that pops into your head. Without any hesitation or even thinking about it, I found myself writing, "my family" for both answers. It was only later after doing some proper self-reflection that I understood why my family is both a strength and a weakness.

The strength part was fairly obvious: They are my biggest driving force for success. Every day, I want to be a better person for my wife and a better father for my baby. I would do anything to protect them. Seeing them happy and thriving is a massive motivator for me. So, why would I then also consider them to be my biggest weakness? Eventually, I understood that it was for the exact same reason: Since they are my main motivators to becoming the best possible version of myself, I felt like I was letting them down when I experienced setbacks or made mistakes. And, since I'm only human, mistakes and challenges are part of my daily life. I felt like I was doomed to fail my family.

My wife could see I was dealing with a lot of inner conflict. One night after the kids were both in bed, we had a long discussion about this. She helped me understand that the deep feelings I have for my family are one of the most beautiful things, even though it makes me feel weak at times. She also reminded me that even though being a father and a husband are the most important roles in my life, I was also a human being.

This whole experience reminded us both of the importance of living a balanced life. You can't be so overly focused on doing right by your family that you neglect yourself. On the flip side of the coin, you also can't become selfish and only do things for yourself. The coin toss between life and fatherhood is all about striking the perfect balance. Unfortunately, I often found it easier to find this balance on a seesaw with my 180-pound body on one side and my 40-pound son on the other. You can't manipulate the seesaw of life by keeping your weight-bearing feet on the ground as you can on the playground.

I was lucky to have my wife's full support in trying to find this perfect balance. Together, we worked on various strategies to not only find pockets of "me time" during the day for both of us but also to bring the spark back to our relationship and make time for friends. We also decided on implementing strict boundaries, with each other, our extended family, our friends, and work colleagues. I know it sounds like a lot, but I quickly learned communication is key.

REDISCOVERING PERSONAL SPACE: FINDING POCKETS OF "ME TIME"

Being the hands-on father I know you are (or will be), it can be difficult to even imagine taking time for yourself, let alone actually doing it. Let me tell you how my brain would operate, every day before work, I would help get everything ready in the house and for our baby. The same goes for after work: I do my part in the kitchen helping to prepare dinner and clean up afterward. I always tried to make time to play with the baby. Then, I took care of bathing the baby. And my wife and I would alternate putting our little one to sleep. I remember thinking it would be impossible to fit in "me time;" my schedule was just too busy.

However, my wife and I both realized how important it is to remain an individual and not just a parent. To do this, we decided to focus on the quality of the "me time," not the length of time. Because, let's face it, scraping ten minutes for yourself is a lot easier than hoping for a full hour solo. These are some of the strategies we implemented to find these pockets of "me time":

Think or journal about what "me time" means to you: Every person will have their own idea of "me time" and how they want to use it. Consider what you regard as "time well spent" and how you can do more of that in your life. It can be helpful to make a list of different short activities you can try to bring into this time.

Always have a shower: I know this might sound ridiculous but when you're consumed with parenting tasks, making time to clean yourself might not be at the top of your list. But, if you're able to make time for this, you will not only feel better about yourself but also get a few minutes of self-care. If you don't have anyone to watch your baby while you shower, you can put them in a rocking or vibrating chair with you in the bathroom.

Shop while they are sleeping: If you need to do some shopping, try to do it while your baby's sleeping peacefully in their stroller. There is probably nothing worse than having to walk through shops with a crying baby. But, if they are able to sleep sweet and sound, you can enjoy the experience a lot more. The movement of the stroller will likely at the same time help rock them to stay asleep for longer.

Catch up while you feed: While you're feeding your baby, you'll spend a lot of time seated. Why not use this time to relax and binge your favorite show or listen to a podcast while you're feeding your baby? This can, therefore, double as precious "me time" as well.

Use nap times to relax: We often try to rush through our chores while the baby is asleep. When they awake, we are left feeling exhausted by the time they wake up and need our attention again. Create a rule that this time should only be used for relaxing activities. If you do, you'll feel more energized when your baby wakes up. When our children were babies, we made peace with the fact that our house didn't look perfect. We just reminded ourselves that guests came to visit us and see our baby, not to judge us for the state of our house.

See your time as being more valuable than money: While you can always take out a loan if you need extra money, you can't ever do this with time, so think about how you want to spend your time. If you have ten minutes to spare, what would you like to do to get the most out of the time?

Destroy time wasters: We all have little habits that waste our time. This can be playing games on our phones or checking social media every few minutes. If we can identify these time wasters and work to reduce them, we'll potentially gain a lot more time to spend on more relaxing or valuable activities.

Add "me time" to your schedule: One of the best ways of making sure you get time to relax is to schedule it. This way your partner will also be on the same page when you're going to enjoy a few minutes by yourself, which will help her to plan your baby's routine accordingly. Always remember to also add some "me time" for your partner to the schedule so she can also enjoy time by herself to relax.

Be sure that you have realistic expectations when it comes to finding pockets of "me time." You can't expect to suddenly have hours of time to yourself when your partner and baby need you.

STRENGTHENING YOUR RELATIONSHIP: KEEPING THE SPARK ALIVE

As I've mentioned a few times, becoming a parents will change your relationship with your partner. No matter how much you might live in a dream world where becoming parents won't impact your connection, it's just not realistic. Where you could spend as much time alone together as you both wanted to, your days will now revolve around your little one. However, this doesn't have to be negative. In fact, I know many couples who make it through parenting an infant stronger than ever before. Luckily, there are many ways in which you can work on keeping the spark alive in your intimate relationship. These are some of the strategies we implemented:

- **Discuss your parenting views:** If you and your partner are on the same page on how you want to parent your baby, you'll avoid a lot of unnecessary conflict in your relationship. This can also increase the trust you have in your co-parent, as you'll know that any decisions to be made when you're not around will be in alignment. Some hot topics you should discuss can include discipline, education, religion, and access your extended family should have with your baby.

- **Multi-tasking time:** You're likely used to spending a lot of time together as a couple, but this will change when you become a parent. Instead of it just being the two of you, you'll now be a family of three or more. However, having an extra human being around shouldn't mean that you and your partner can't connect. All it takes is to use the time you do have more effectively. How can you two do this? For example, my wife and I would have deep discussions while feeding the baby or even doing chores around the house. We realized that if you're both invested, not just in the relationship but also in the conversation, you don't have to sit still to have a meaningful discussion.
- **Talk about your finances:** There aren't a lot of things that can result in arguments quite like different views on finances. But, if you and your partner are in agreement with how you'll spend your money and have budgets in place, you'll be better prepared for when all the unexpected expenses that a baby can bring come your way. We created a rule where we decided on a set amount of money per month and agreed that before spending a cent more, we'd discuss it first. This helped to increase the trust and appreciation in our relationship.
- **Look to the future:** Another thing you and your partner should continuously be talking about is your hopes and dreams for the future. This will be extremely valuable if you communicate well. Sharing your future plans will help remind you of

everything you have to look forward to. It will give you both hope that you'll survive the chaos that life with a newborn can bring and that you can even get to the other side stronger than ever before.

- **Connect intimately:** Fellas, your eyes probably lit up now thinking that I'm referring to having sex again. Yes, I do believe sex is important in every relationship, it shouldn't be the be-all and end-all of your intimacy with your partner. She has been through a physical and emotional rollercoaster to give you a baby. Even if the six weeks that most doctors recommend new mothers abstain from sex post-birth is over, it doesn't mean your partner will be ready to become sexually active again. Look at other ways of being more intimate with your partner that won't necessarily lead to a happy ending. Hold your partner's hand, massage her back, or cuddle with her on the couch to remain connected. Perhaps, watch a throwback movie to when you first met. Tune into your teenage self and just enjoy the rush that other levels of intimacy can bring.

- **My new dad friends, I'm not going to lie to you:** There were a few times when I thought my marriage wouldn't survive the newborn phases. Now that my children are bigger, I can honestly say our marriage didn't just make it through these challenging times, but we thrived because of them. I am forever grateful to my wife, not just for helping me create our beautiful children but also for being willing to work with me on strengthening our bond.

We are a team. And, let me be the first to tell you that I am not perfect. So, the fact that she's willing to practice patience with me too, is a blessing in itself. When we got married, we promised, "Until death do us part." We did everything we could to make sure that doesn't change to, "Until newborn do us part."

INTEGRATING FRIENDS AND SOCIAL LIFE INTO FATHERHOOD

Just as your relationship with your partner will change once you become a parent, your connections with your friends can also suffer due to the demands of fatherhood. I am a complete extrovert and always had large groups of friends. Unfortunately, I only discovered after the birth of our son that they were more "good time" friends than good friends. When I couldn't meet them as much as I used to anymore, their interest in my life seemed to play a disappearing act on me. Or as the kids nowadays call it (including my own), I got "ghosted."

As much as this frustrated me, I decided to focus on my family. For a while, I was so consumed by slotting into my new role that my heavily declining social life didn't bother me as much. However, as my baby grew and I gained a bit more free time, I was desperate for some time with my buddies again. Judging by my wife's encouragement to reconnect with some of my friends, I'm sure she could also do with me getting a boost from some social interaction.

Unfortunately, I had no idea how to restart my social life again. I've never been in a position where I had to reach out to and potentially be rejected by friends. It always came so naturally, so putting myself out there again (first time since high school) was new territory for me. These are some of the steps I took to reach out and regain my social life:

- **Reconnecting with old buddies:** I started by contacting my old friends one by one. I did this over messaging and since I wanted to send personalized messages to them instead of just copying and pasting a mass message, it was quite a time-consuming task. I used my "me time" moments to do this, as well as while feeding my little one. I started these messages by telling them what was happening in my life, how I've survived the newborn phase, and how I missed hanging out. For those friends who were fathers, I added some information on my baby but didn't want to bore the childless friends with an overload of baby pictures. Then, I asked about how they were doing. I resisted the urge to immediately invite them for a quick lunch or game of golf. Instead, I used this time just to check in.

- **Recall memories:** I went through some of my old photos and created a folder on my laptop where I copied some of my best memories with friends. Once this was done, I posted a photo every other day on my social media accounts and tagged them in it. Some of the pics that might have been a bit more "early days college-themed," I forwarded privately to them. This helped to open the conversation of reminiscing together, which eventually led to lines such as, "It would be great to catch up!"

- **Set up a get-together:** Eventually, messages turned into phone calls. Before I knew it, we connected again, and I had a few lunches marked on the calendar. My father took my wife and baby out on a relaxing day, which was a nice bonding for them. It was great knowing that I didn't have to worry about them at home or rush back to help out. I might have been a little nervous beforehand, not going to lie. But, once we met at the lunch spot, it was like no time had passed.

- **Find a common interest:** One of my old friends is a sports freak just like me. His baby is actually only a few months older than my son, so we have a lot of similarities in our lives. Our wives also used to get on like a house on fire. As a result, I thought he would be a fantastic person to form a deeper friendship with. There was a half-marathon coming up in our city in a few months and even though neither of us were runners, I saw this as a golden opportunity. After convincing him to enter the race with me, we started training together. This didn't mean that we would go for runs every day; our schedules didn't allow for this. Instead, we mostly trained separately in our own time but would share our training performances with each other. This common goal was a fantastic re-entry point to what is now one of my best friendships.

- **Connect while you're at home:** Another friend of mine is big into gaming. I've never really been a gamer, but I had an Xbox at home. I saw on Facebook that he really enjoys a specific game, so I asked him more about it. Eventually, he offered to help me get started. We connected our Xboxes and played together online. I did this while my son was happily playing with his toys right next to me. I'll admit, I didn't become a full-on gamer like some of those YouTubers, but I now can play a mean game of FIFA.

- **Join online groups:** While I was posting photos on Facebook, I wondered if there weren't any first-time dad groups I could join. I mean, there are groups for literally everything on Facebook. After a quick search, I joined a few groups. What a great idea that was! I could connect with other first-time dads from the comfort of my child's play mat. Not only did I learn many hacks on these groups, but it was also great to know that other first-time dads also wondered why their babies would play with a dead worm that they had found in the grass. It was fantastic to know we weren't quite as odd as I started to suspect.

Apart from these tips, I also learned to forgive and forget small things that happened in the past. There was no reason for me to still be upset over an old friend who got the girl I was after 15 years ago. I should actually thank him because if he didn't also pursue her, I might never have met my wife.

Giving up past hurts and arguments made me more suscep-tible to new friendships.

SETTING BOUNDARIES: NAVIGATING ADVICE AND RELATIVES

As I worked on expanding our circle of friends, I became more and more aware of the need to have proper boundaries in place to protect myself and my new family. These boundaries were not just for my friends but for my relatives as well. I had an aunt who would just pop by unannounced to spend time with the baby. As much as we appreciated the love she had for him, I can't tell you how many times I had to run to the room to get dressed suddenly while she was standing at our front door. Because, yes, my fellow new dads, there are many Saturday mornings that I sit in the living room wearing only my boxers.

Healthy boundaries are all about making sure you only allow things to enter your life that you're truly comfortable with. Doing the sprints in my underwear to the room while my aunt was in the house wasn't something that would fall in my comfort zone. I had to sit my aunt down and explain to her that as much as we love her presence in our lives and appreciate the love she showed our son, she needed to communicate to us when she wanted to visit and not just show up. At first, I could see she took offense as she believed a person shouldn't have to create a formal meeting to see family, let alone her nephew. But, she saw I wasn't budging on the boundary, so she had to comply.

This is just one example of the many boundaries we created to make our lives easier and to protect us from unwanted (or embarrassing) situations. I urge you to think about your life and make a list of the things you're either uncomfortable with or absolutely don't want in your life. Remember, this is your life so even if you feel it may be selfish, don't ignore your feelings. The person you're creating the boundary for will rarely be happy with the limitations you're setting, so make peace with that and do what's right for you and your family.

Once you have your list of the unwanted behaviors or circumstances you want to avoid, think about the boundary you want to set. What changed behaviors or circumstances would you be willing to accept? What boundaries can be set to enforce this? Also, since the other person will likely object to these, decide beforehand which of your new limits are non-negotiables, and how far you're willing to compromise on the others.

After you've created your list of boundaries, you need to discuss these with the other people involved. Explain to them honestly why you can't allow their behavior to continue and what you expect from them going forward. Remember that you can't expect these people to smell that you've created a boundary, as if a boundary needs to be set, clearly there is a disconnect to begin with there. If you don't tell them, they'll never know that they should change their behavior. If you're discussing a boundary that is non-negotiable. Where you are willing to compromise, listen to them, give your feedback, and see how you can decide on a way forward together. If you need time to think after listening to their point of view, explain that so you can problem-solve with them.

You can follow these steps in any situation, from setting boundaries with your partner, your child (when they are older), your family and friends, and even your boss or work colleagues. Always remember you have the right to stand up for yourself and what you want in your life. Don't be the fool that I was that had to run around the house in your undies unless that's something you enjoy, of course!

TEST YOUR NEW DAD IQ: CHAPTER 6

Finding the balance in your new life can be tricky, especially if you're still getting used to your role as a first-time dad. But, let me tell you, once you're able to navigate the seesaw without needing to put your feet on the ground for support, you'll find so much more enjoyment in life than you might have thought possible. Before we move on to the final chapter, let's do a quick check to test your new dad's IQ. If you struggle with any of these questions, refer back to the various sections in the chapter to refresh your memory.

1. **Why is it important that you and your partner are on the same page in terms of parenting values?**
2. **Can I set boundaries without communicating with the other person?**
3. **Once your partner reaches the big six-week postpartum milestone, is it okay to expect her to resume intimacy?**

4. If you've lost contact with many of your old friends during the newborn stage, should you just give up on having friends again?
5. Do you need hours by yourself for "me time?"

While balancing the new and old parts of your life, there's another essential aspect we mustn't forget: Capturing the fleeting moments of your baby's growth. In the next chapter, dive deep into the world of documenting milestones and creating beautiful memories to cherish forever. We'll also cast our gaze further and discuss what lies beyond these initial 365 days of your baby's life.

CHAPTER SEVEN

DOCUMENTING MILESTONES AND LOOKING AHEAD

You've probably heard the famous saying that even though the days are long, the years can be short many times before. Never have I found this to be as true and applicable as in parenthood. There are days when you literally want to run for the hills to escape. First from your newborn's cries, then your toddler's tantrums, your elementary school's principal, and finally, your teenager's mood swings. Trust me, fellas, it doesn't always get easier as your child grows up.

However, just as long as your days can sometimes feel, so short are the years. I remember many people telling me to appreciate every second of fatherhood as they grow up so quickly, but I never truly understood how quickly the years would fly by. It feels like I blinked and my firstborn son was ready for school.

Even though you make memories every day in raising your child, you won't remember half of them. These amazing times that should make fantastic memories come so quickly and fast that it can honestly be difficult to keep track of all of them. My wife was good at always keeping her phone with her and capturing as many memories as she could. She took amazing photos and videos of me playing with our little one. Unfortunately, since she was always behind the lens, I never even thought of taking photos of her with our son. I wasn't earning an Oscar for my director skills.

To try to help get you in the running for this imaginary award, we'll now discuss the importance of capturing memories (and making sure your partner also features in these photos). I'll also give you tips a photographer friend of mine gave me when I tried to rectify my mistakes with our second child. These tips will help take your photos from "meh" to "blow up and put on the wall" art pieces, even if you're only using your phone's camera.

We'll also look beyond the first year to the terror that can come with toddlerhood. Fear not, every stage comes with breathtakingly joyful moments.

THE IMPORTANCE OF CAPTURING FIRSTS

Take a moment to think of your favorite memories on your parenting journey so far. Allow me to take a guess: Depending on where you are on your journey, these memories most likely include the day you found out your partner was pregnant, the day you first heard your baby's heartbeat on an ultrasound scan, definitely the day your little one was born, and perhaps already a few others.

When we are emotional, our memories are processed differently in our brains—neurons in the amygdala activate during emotional responses—making them more clear and longer lasting. These can be positive and negative feelings, which is why traumatic experiences can be just as vivid in your memory as positive ones. When you find a reminder of a positive experience, such as a photo of one of your baby's first smiles or their belly laughs, it brings back the strong emotions you experienced during that event, which will help you remember that wonderful moment with a lot more clarity.

I experienced this the other day when a friend of mine, who is about to have his first baby, asked me about the birth of our children. I told him as much as I could remember, but to be honest, I was shocked at how vague my memory was. I could recall the big moments but those small things that were so precious to me at the time were rusty in my memory. That night, I took out the old photo albums (my wife prefers to have old-school hardcopy photo albums, not just digital ones) and as I looked through the photos, the memories of those amazing moments flushed back. I felt just as emotional as I did the day I first heard my son's first cries.

My wife and I spent hours looking at the photos and recalling stories. If it wasn't for the photos, so many of those memories would be lost. Again, I was featured like a super dad in those photos, since my wife took most of them. The lack of photos of my wife was so evident that she even joked that it looked like I was a single dad. She thought her joke was very funny. I didn't. I wished I could have a time machine. Fellas, I'll say it again. Learn from my mistakes and take photos of your partner with your baby. She will thank you for it.

TIPS FOR TAKING MEMORABLE PHOTOS

As I've mentioned, after I realized my blunder in not taking photos of my wife with our baby, I really wanted to step it up when our daughter was born. Luckily, I have a very successful photographer friend, Annika. I asked her for some tips on taking the best possible photos using just my cell phone. I really wanted to impress. And, I did. We now have an album filled with photos of my wife, our newborn daughter, and the proud big brother (at the time of writing this book we only had 2 kids to our name, oh how that has changed). In fact, now it looked as if my wife was a single mom.

To help you gain confidence behind the camera to capture beautiful images of your little one, I'll now share Annika's amazing tips:

- **Go down to their level:** Too many pictures of little children are taken from above from your height. Not only do children look fairly awkward (their head is closer to the camera lens, so it naturally seems too big for their body), but they also won't be comfortable. If you bend down to take the picture from the front, their bodies will be proportionate and since you won't stand in front of them as an imposing figure, they will be more at ease. You'll not only get better reactions and facial expressions out of them but you'll also see their faces a lot more clearly in the photos.

- **Take more than one picture:** Camera phones capture images fairly quickly, which makes it easy to take multiple pictures in a single go. If you have an iPhone, you can hold down the button to take batches of photos at lightning speed. Use this to your advantage and take a few pictures from different angles. If you can, move around so that not all the photos are from the front view. Sometimes, side-view photos can be exceptionally powerful. Don't forget about the zoom function when you take these pictures. Your first photo could be the ultimate winner, but you never know what treasures you might capture if you just take a few more.

- **Grab a bag of patience:** Young babies are the perfect photography models as they have no choice but to lie still for as long as you need them to. Toddlers, however, are on the complete opposite side of the scale. They often don't want to sit still, smile, or cooperate in any way. Unfortunately, you'll have to push through and make something work if you want your older child to also feature in photos. Annika is all about taking "candid" photos, not posed ones, which is actually perfect for photographing a toddler. Just sit patiently with your camera ready to capture. When they do something cute, click immediately. Trust me, they move fast so you won't have a lot of time. If you missed the shot, just wait until they either do it again or do something else (perhaps even better than your first try). However, don't ask them to do what they just did again. Trust me, new dads, you'll most likely end up with a tantrum.

- **Look for natural light:** If you are in a room with natural light coming in through a window, place the person you want to take a photo of close to that window. This way the natural light will shine on the person's face, improving the quality of the image drastically. If you want to take photos of a difficult subject (again, think toddler), encourage them to play close to the window while you snap them without them realizing you're taking a photo.

- **Always look at the background:** I'm sure you've seen those photos of someone sitting on a park bench with a massive tree branch growing out of their head. If the person in the photo just moved a few inches to the side, this same branch could've framed them beautifully. When you want to encourage your child to play somewhere with enough natural light, first look at the background. Remember, it's best to move your toddler once to avoid them having a meltdown. If you only realized that there's something in the background and your child isn't in the mood to be moved, consider changing your angle.

- **There's a dinosaur above my head:** Have you ever looked at pictures of young children and wondered why their smiles like so exceptionally fake or even skewed when they usually have the sweetest smile? Annika believes that in most of these cases, the photographer prompted them with the age-old habit, "Say cheese!" Instead of trying to get your child to smile on demand, do something that will make them give a genuine smile or even laugh. You can do faces, make funny sounds, or as worked best with my son, tell them, "There's a dinosaur above my head!" This way, I got him to even look in the camera's direction; double bonus. If these tricks don't work, moody or serious facial expressions can sometimes make even better photos than the typical smiles. Otherwise, just remain ready, armed with your bag full of patience. Eventually, you'll get a real smile out of them.
- **Take photos in .5:** If you're using an iPhone, you can use the .5 setting on your phone to capture more of the setting. It really is a cool hack. If you're using an Android phone, play around with the different options in the phone's camera. You'll be surprised at the amazing photos these little gadgets can take.

Sometimes, even if you follow all these tips, it's just not possible to take that perfect picture you want to hang on your wall. So, I have to share this story with you. While I was in my photography craze after the birth of our daughter in the hopes of scoring serious brownie points, my sister came to visit with her son. He was just over three years old at the time, and if you look up the explanation of the phrase "terrifying toddler" in the dictionary, you'll see a picture of him there. Just joking, of course, but he could throw a meltdown like no other.

I really wanted to get a picture of our children with their cousin, but he just wouldn't cooperate. He kept on screaming something that I honestly couldn't understand. My sister eventually told me to stop trying. He just wouldn't stop crying. After standing dumbfounded for a few minutes, I decided to just go with it. By that time, he knew too well that I tried to take a photo of him, so we ended up with photos of my baby lying there (because she had no choice), my son using her tummy as a track for his little toy car, and the cousin crying in the background. And, you know what, those are now some of our favorite photos and are not just up on the wall in our house, but in my sister's as well.

PREPARING FOR THE TODDLER STAGE

You've likely heard of toddler tantrums before, seen them in the lines at shops, or got scared reading about my nephew above. Unfortunately, once your baby grows into this phase, it's too late to get scared of a little meltdown. Now, you just need to power through. Luckily, it doesn't last very long, but there is a reason why people refer to these ages as the "terrible twos" and "terrifying threes."

These little humans are growing fast and learning to do new things every day. They typically know exactly what they want and their willpower is second to none. Unfortunately, their brain development often lags behind their physical abilities. This can result in them desperately wanting to do something, but lacking the words to explain their wants and needs to you. If you don't immediately know what their disjointed mumbles mean, they get upset. I mean, let's face it, you would also get upset when you believe you explain yourself perfectly to another person, and they just don't seem to understand you.

Their little bodies and brains don't know how to cope with these extremely intense emotions. As a result, they have a meltdown, which can result in uncontrollable crying, throwing their bodies down onto the floor in frustration, or even hurting themselves. Remember, they don't mean to be the terrifying little monsters that they appear to be. They just can't think of better ways of showing you that they are upset.

Luckily, toddlerhood isn't all bad. Not even close to all bad. This is an amazing time when you'll be astounded on a daily basis by the incredible development your child is showing. They'll start to talk in short little sentences. You probably already can't wait to have full-on conversations with your baby. But, be careful what you wish for. On some days, it feels as if my pocket rocket of a daughter tries to say all the words in the dictionary at least six times. There's never a quiet moment with her in the vicinity.

Your child's physical skills will also improve. Soon, your little baby will be running around climbing on everything they see. Yes, my new dad friends, your heart will skip a few beats as you watch your little one try gravity-defying jumps off a jungle gym. Some days I wished those capes my son loved to wear pretending to be Superman, would really turn him into a superhero so that my heart could have a little vacation.

They will slowly but surely become more independent. I won't ever forget the day my wife phoned me while I was still at work. She was so excited that I could barely hear a word she said. Apparently, my son just finished making his own peanut butter and jelly sandwich. It's those little moments in life that turn into the big ones. I must admit, I felt both proud and a little sad when I heard he was such a "big boy" to make his own lunch. My baby boy most definitely wasn't a baby anymore.

The third book in my series, *You Will Rock as a Dad: 85 New Dad Toddler Hacks* The Easy-To-Implement Modern Dad Cheatsheet will uncover everything you need to know about toddlerhood: The good, the bad, and downright ugly tantrums. I will share all the amazing strategies and techniques that helped us survive and thrive through this stage. Together, we can continue our amazing teamwork that helped you rock as a dad during pregnancy and the first year of your baby's life.

TEST YOUR NEW DAD IQ: CHAPTER 7

Time flies when you're having fun, and also when you're raising children. No matter how difficult some days might be, they will soon be a distant memory that you wish you could relive. Yes, chaps, soon you'll even wish you could have those bad days again. That is how amazing fatherhood is. Since no one has successfully invented a time travel machine yet (or at least, not that I know of), you'll have to rely on your memories to reminisce about past milestones. So, let's test your new dad IQ to make sure you capture these moments properly (unlike I did with my firstborn). If you struggle with any of these questions, refer back to the various sections in the chapter to refresh your memory.

1. **Why do we remember emotional memories much more clearly?**
2. **How can you ensure your photos have adequate natural light?**
3. **What often happens when you tell a young child to "say cheese"?**
4. **Why is it important to make sure your partner is in many of the photos?**
5. **If your child doesn't want to sit still for a photo, is it okay to tie them to a chair? (I am absolutely joking. Please don't think I tie my children to chairs!)**

As we wrap up this guide, remember that fatherhood isn't just about the destination but the journey. Each chapter of your child's life brings its unique set of challenges and joys. As you've navigated the first year, take a moment to reflect on the beautiful journey ahead.

CONCLUSION

This first year is just the opening chapter to an epic tale of fatherhood. As you've navigated the initial joys and challenges, know that every moment, every stumble, every triumph is shaping you into an even better father. Soon, you'll rock at this little old thing called fatherhood, if you aren't already.

Life with a newborn can be tough on even the emotionally strongest people. But, if you make sure you set the right expectations, learn the power of patience, with your baby and your partner who has just been through thick and thin to bring your child to life, and focus on doing the basics right while focusing on what you can control, you'll get through it with flying colors.

Being a dad doesn't just mean you've impregnated your partner. It means sharing the responsibilities. Those dirty diapers won't clean themselves. Even if you have to swallow your vomit ten times cleaning up a poop explosion or dodging the fountains that boys can make, you can do it. I know you can. Remember, even though breast milk is considered golden milk for your baby, it's more important to just make sure your little one is fed. So, if your partner can't breastfeed, get into problem-solving mode. Formula is an excellent alternative to breast milk. Take charge of certain parenting tasks, and use these moments with your baby as the precious bonding experiences that they can and should be. Remember, bonding isn't just a maternal thing.

Always keep an eye out for any health concerns in your baby. Many of these can easily be treated at home, so if you're ever unsure, refer back to Chapter 5 for tips. But, remember, pediatricians are trained not only in treating illness in babies but also in dealing with terrified first-time parents. So, if you want the reassurance that the pimple on your baby's cheek is only baby acne, don't hesitate to take it. As the saying goes, prevention is always better than cure. Also, refer back to the health red flags we discussed in this chapter and take your baby for a thorough checkup if you're ever concerned about any of them.

Remember to try to find the perfect balance in your life between being a father, a partner, and an individual. When you need to, steal a pocket of "me time," but remember to encourage your partner to do the same. She will most likely also be desperate for some time by herself, even if it's just a few minutes. Never disregard the impact that "New Dad Anxiety" can have, not only in your life but also in the lives of your partner and baby. Having emotions and experiencing anxiety doesn't make you weak. Instead, communicating your feelings and that you may be struggling is one of the biggest signs of strength.

Cherish every moment of your journey through fatherhood, even the less-than-desirable ones! Remember to capture as many experiences as you can, and make sure your partner is also in the photos. Time flies, and before you know it, your little one won't be so little anymore. Embrace every second, every giggle, and even every midnight wake-up call. These are the moments that mold your legacy.

TEST YOUR NEW DAD IQ: REFLECT ON FATHERHOOD

Once you get closer to your baby's first birthday, I want to encourage you to take some time to reflect on your journey through fatherhood this far. If it's still a few months to go, grab your phone and set a reminder to get back to this section. Reflection is extremely important to help you realize how far you've come since those octopus days when you felt too uncoordinated to hold your baby. I'm convinced that you'll be absolutely amazed at the progress you've made, and realize that you truly deserve to wear your own super dad cape with pride.

I used to often postpone (or even put off) doing proper self-reflection, believing that there were more important things to do with my time. Then, I came across a quote by Canadian author Robin Sharma who famously wrote, "Awareness precedes choice and choice precedes change" (Sharma, n.d.). If we want to deliberately act in positive or helpful ways, we must make choices to support those actions. And, to make those choices, we need greater awareness of ourselves and our lives. I firmly believe practicing self-reflection and becoming more aware of both the positives and negatives in my life have helped me to become a better father, husband, and friend.

If you feel unsure of how to reflect on your amazing journey through the first year of fatherhood, take a moment to consider the man you were before your child's birth and the father you've become. Reflect on the shifts in your perspectives, priorities, and emotions. Use the prompts below to guide your introspection:

Before, now, and the future:

- Describe yourself in three words before your child was born.
- Now, choose three words that describe you as a father today.
- When you reflect on your journey in a year's time (when your child is two), which three words do you hope will describe you?
- What actions (if any) do you plan to take to get you closer to these three words?

Proudest moments:

- Jot down one specific instance where you felt immense pride in your role as a dad.
- What contributed to this proud moment?
- If you have anyone specific to thank for helping you create this moment, do so now. Even if this

moment happened months ago and they might not remember their input, you should still consider showing gratitude for the people on your journey.

Challenges overcame:

- Think of a difficult moment you've successfully navigated. What did it teach you?
- How did you overcome this challenge?
- If you were to face a similar struggle in the future, how would you tackle it?

Shift in priorities:

- List one thing that used to be crucial to you but has taken a backseat since becoming a father. How did this impact your life?
- What other things should you prioritize in the year ahead?

Emotional evolution:

- Describe an emotion or feeling you've only experienced since your child's birth.
- Have you become more comfortable with your emotions over this past year? If so, how?
- Are you still experiencing "New Dad Anxiety?" If not, how did you overcome it?

Fatherhood isn't a destination; it's a continuous voyage. You're equipped, you're prepared, and most importantly, you will rock as a dad! Keep growing, keep learning, and above all, keep loving. The adventure has only just begun.

If you enjoyed reading this book and found the information helpful in preparation for your journey, please leave us a 5-star review on Amazon, as your feedback can help another first-time father who is at the start of his journey, like you once were. Also, be sure to keep an eye out for my next and 3rd book, *You Will Rock as a Dad!: 85 New Dad Toddler Hacks* The Easy-To-Implement Modern Dad Cheatsheet so that we can keep going on the journey of fatherhood together.

Thank you for coming on this journey with me once again.

Keep up that "rockin' dad energy"

Your friend,

~ Alex

REFERENCES

Ben-Joseph, E. P. (2018, June). Breastfeeding vs. formula feeding (for parents). *Kidshealth*. https://kidshealth.org/en/parents/breast-bottle-feeding.html

Benefits of tummy time. *(n.d.). Safe to Sleep*. https://safetosleep.nichd.nih.gov/reduce-risk/tummy-time

BetterHelp Editorial Team. (2024, January 25). Understanding the facts about emotional memory. *BetterHelp*. https://www.betterhelp.com/advice/memory/understanding-the-facts-about-emotional-memory/

Bonding and attachment: Newborns. *(2023, May 26). Raising Children Network.* https://raisingchildren.net.au/newborns/connecting-communicating/bonding/bonding-newborns

Breastfeeding: How partners can help. *(2022, October 11). Raising Children Network.* https://raisingchildren.net.au/pregnancy/pregnancy-for-partners/early-parenting/breastfeeding-partners-can-help

Brindle, D. (1999, June 16). Fathers under pressure to become superdads. *The Guardian*. https://www.theguardian.com/uk/1999/jun/16/davidbrindle

Canfield, K. (2007, April 27). Dads of toddlers need patience. *National Center for Fathering*. https://fathers.com/blog/your-kids/preschoolers/dads-of-toddlers-need-patience/

Canzater, S. L. (2019, July 11). Talk to me, baby! The benefits of frequent, high-quality conversations with babies on brain and language development. *O'Neill Institute*. https://oneill.law.georgetown.edu/talk-to-me-baby-the-benefits-of-frequent-high-quality-conversations-with-babies-on-brain-and-language-development/

CDC. (2021, February 22). Toddlers (1-2 years old). *Centers for Disease Control and Prevention*. https://www.cdc.gov/ncbddd/childdevelopment/positiveparenting/toddlers.html

FamilyEducation Editorial Staff. (2022, January 12). Pressures of modern dads. *FamilyEducation*. https://www.familyeducation.com/family-life/work/unique-pressures-21st-century-dad

5 natural diaper rash remedies that actually work. *(n.d.). Mustela*. https://www.mustelausa.com/blogs/mustela-mag/natural-diaper-rash-remedies

Fontaine, D. (2023, December 22). *12 best natural remedies for eczema*. Medical News Today. https://www.medicalnewstoday.com/articles/324228

Gill, K. (2023, July 23). How to get rid of cradle cap: Home remedies and when to seek help. *Healthline.* https://www.healthline.com/health/parenting/how-to-get-rid-of-cradle-cap

HealthPartners. (2021, May 6). 13 tips for father-baby bonding. *HealthPartners.* https://www.healthpartners.com/blog/tips-for-father-baby-bonding/

Horsager-Boehrer, R. (2021, August 17). *1 in 10 dads experience postpartum depression, anxiety: How to spot the signs. UT Southwestern Medical Center.* https://utswmed.org/medblog/paternal-postpartum-depression/

How many diapers do I need for a newborn? (2020, February 4). Munchkin. https://www.munchkin.com/blog/how-many-diapers-do-i-need-for-a-newborn/

Kreidman, J. (2023, January 20). New dad anxiety - How to overcome the fear of fatherhood. *Dad University.* https://www.daduniversity.com/blog/new-dad-anxiety-how-to-overcome-the-fear-of-fatherhood

Lee, J., Parikka, V., Lehtonen, L., & Soukka, H. (2021). Parent–infant skin-to-skin contact reduces the electrical activity of the diaphragm and stabilizes respiratory function in preterm infants. *Pediatric Research.* https://doi.org/10.1038/s41390-021-01607-2

Marcin, A. (2016, August 3). How to hold a baby: Step by step. *Healthline.* https://www.healthline.com/health/parenting/how-to-hold-a-newborn

Marple, K. (2022). What's your new-father IQ? *BabyCenter.* https://www.babycenter.com/family/fatherhood/new-father-iq_1325162

Mayo Clinic Staff. (2022, January 6). Infant jaundice - Symptoms and causes. *Mayo Clinic.* https://www.mayoclinic.org/diseases-conditions/infant-jaundice/symptoms-causes/syc-20373865

Mayo Clinic Staff. (2023, November 21). Diaper rash - Symptoms and causes. *Mayo Clinic.* https://www.mayoclinic.org/diseases-conditions/diaper-rash/symptoms-causes/syc-20371636

O'Connor, A. (2022, July 14). Vitamins and breastfed babies. *What to Expect.* https://www.whattoexpect.com/first-year/feeding-your-baby/vitamins-and-babies.aspx

Pacheco, D., & Wright, H. (2023, November 16). *Babies and sleep: What to expect & tips.* Sleep Foundation. https://www.sleepfoundation.org/baby-sleep

Patient. (n.d.). *Merriam-Webster.* https://www.merriam-webster.com/dictionary/patient#h1

Pitone, M. (2022, November). *Fevers.* Kids Health. https://kidshealth.org/en/parents/fever.html

Pitone, M. L. (2023, October). *Colic (for parents).* Kids Health. https://kidshealth.org/en/parents/colic.html

Red flags by age for referral of a child. (2021). Help Me Grow. https://helpmegrowm n.org/HMG/GetHelpChild/WhenRefer/RedFlags/index.html

Sharma, R.S. (n.d.) Robin S. Sharma quotes. *Good Reads.* https://www. goodreads.com/quotes/289003-awareness-precedes-choice-and-choice-precedes-change

Skin-to-skin contact with newborns. *(2021, April 6). Pampers.* https://www. pampers.com/en-us/pregnancy/giving-birth/article/skin-to-skin-contact

Storring, C. (2021, October 1). 10 habits and practices to develop mindfulness for dads. Dad.Work. https://dad.work/mindfulness-for-dads/

Tech Team. (2023, June 7). Cloth diapers pros & cons: Cloth vs disposable diapers. *Nicki's Diapers.* https://nickisdiapers.com/blogs/switch-to-sustain able/cloth-diapers-vs-disposable-cost-pros-cons

Tellado, M. P. (2023, September). *Oral thrush.* Kids Health. https://kidshealth. org/en/parents/thrush.html

The Bump Editors. (2018, May 2). Diaper decisions: Cloth diapers vs. disposable. *The Bump.* https://www.thebump.com/a/cloth-diapers-vs-disposable

The importance of celebrating tiny wins as a parent. *(n.d.). Extraordinary Kids Pediatric Therapy Rhode Island.* https://www.extraordinarykidstherapy.net/ blog/the-importance-of-celebrating-tiny-wins-as-a-parent

Toffle, J. (2021, March 30). Embracing imperfection as a parent and what I did about it. *Doctorpedia.* https://www.doctorpedia.com/blog/embracing-imperfection-as-a-parent-and-what-i-did-about-it/

Villano, M. (2018, March 12). When dad struggles after the baby arrives. *Seleni.* https://www.seleni.org/advice-support/2018/3/12/when-dad-struggles-after-the-baby-arrives

www.ingramcontent.com/pod-product-compliance
Lightning Source LLC
Chambersburg PA
CBHW071455140726
47997CB00005B/1732